EASY PIANO

Love Songs of the '20s & '30s

ISBN 0-7935-8339-X

HAL•LEONARD®
CORPORATION

7777 W. BLUEMOUND RD. P.O. BOX 13819 MILWAUKEE, WI 53213

Visit Hal Leonard Online at
www.halleonard.com

Contents

ALL THE THINGS YOU ARE

from VERY WARM FOR MAY

Lyrics by OSCAR HAMMERSTEIN II
Music by JEROME KERN

All that I want in all of this world is you.

Slowly
Burthen*

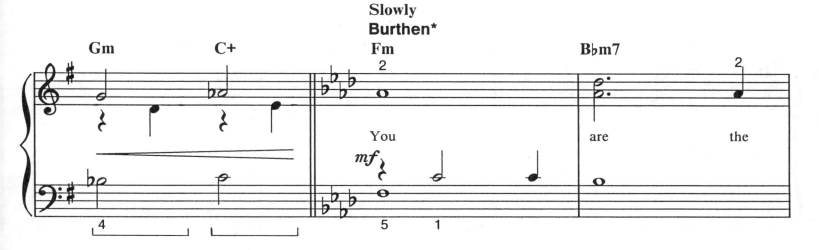

You are the

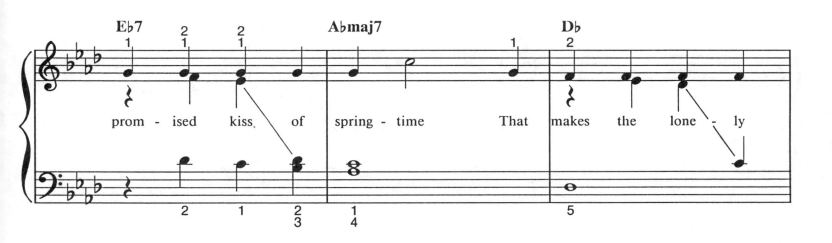

prom - ised kiss of spring - time That makes the lone - ly

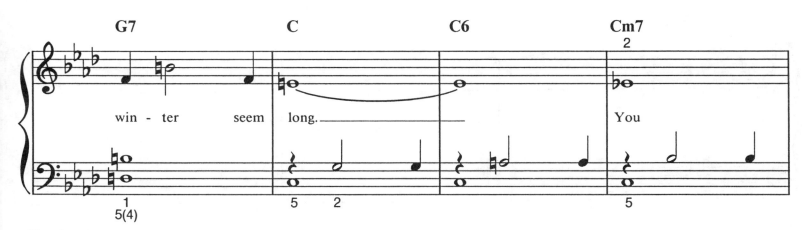

win - ter seem long. You

*Burthen is another word for chorus.

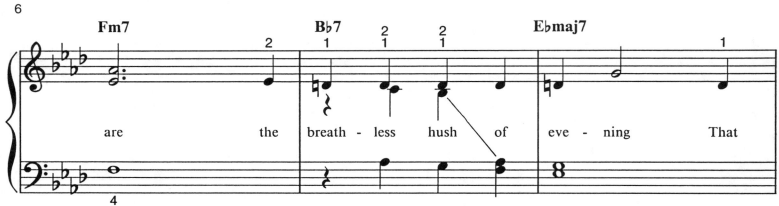

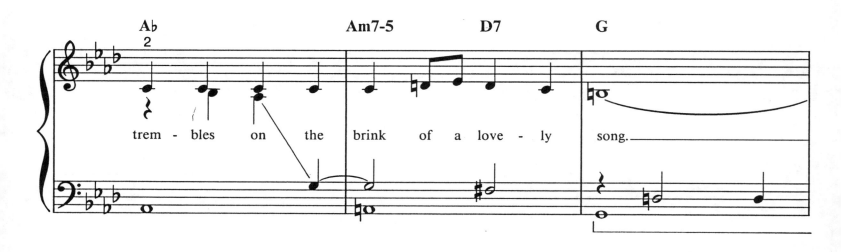

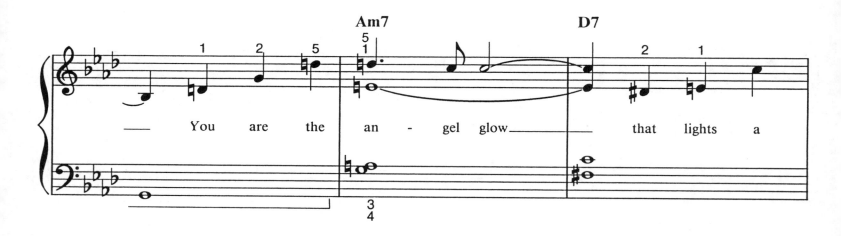

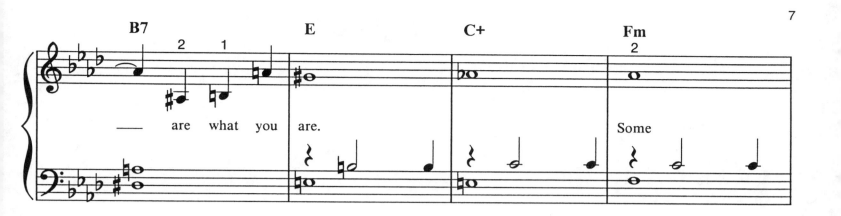

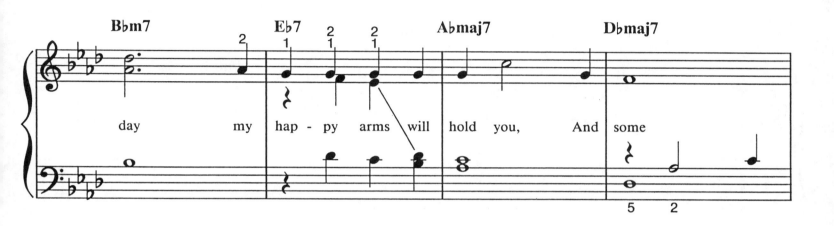

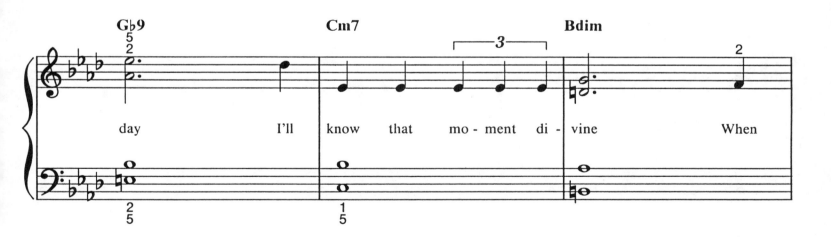

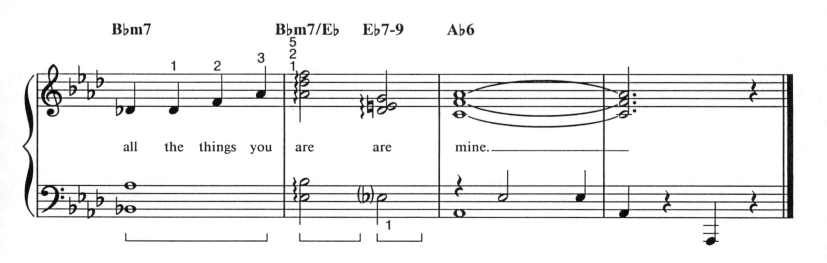

ALWAYS

Words and Music by
IRVING BERLIN

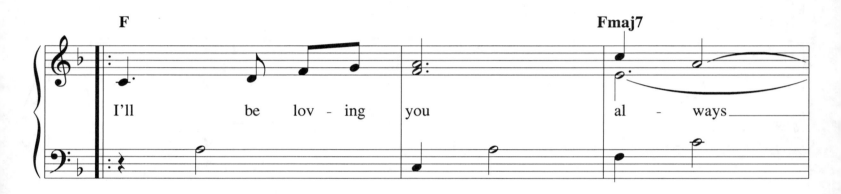

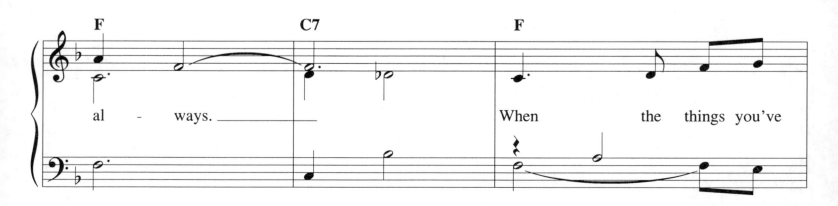

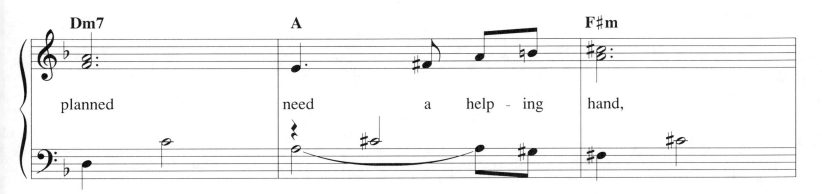

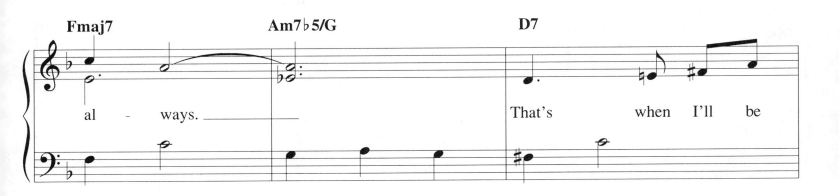

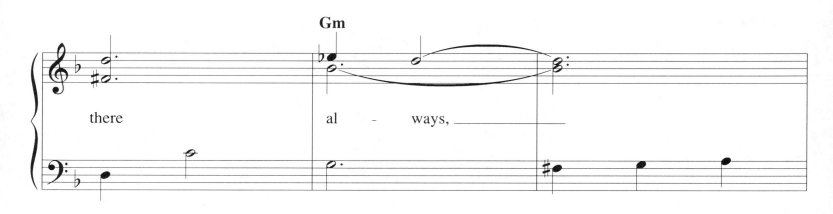

there al - ways, _____

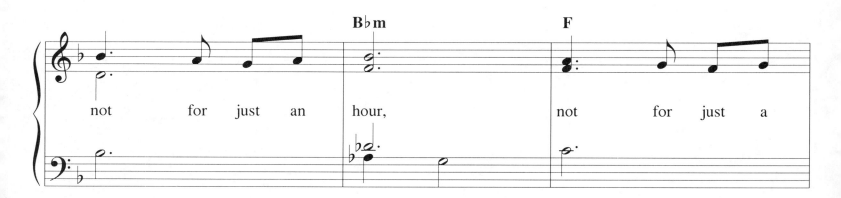

not for just an hour, not for just a

day, not for just a year but al - ways. _____

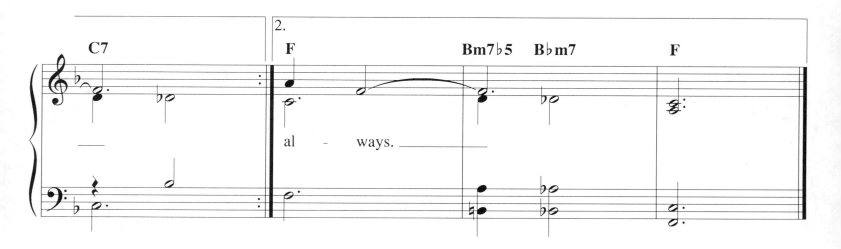

al - ways. _____

ANY TIME

Words and Music by
HERBERT HAPPY LAWSON

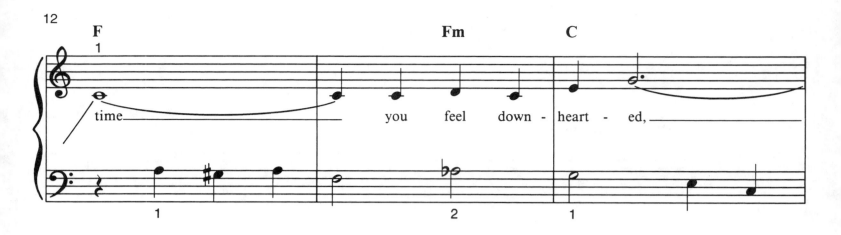

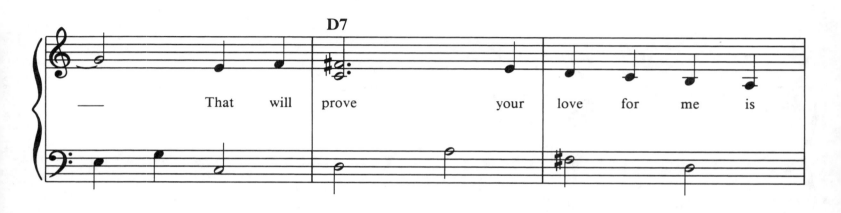

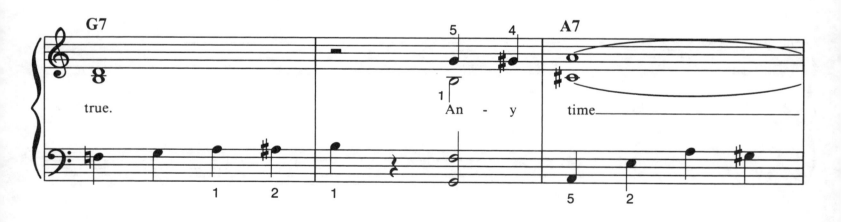

time · · · I'll be think - ing of you. —

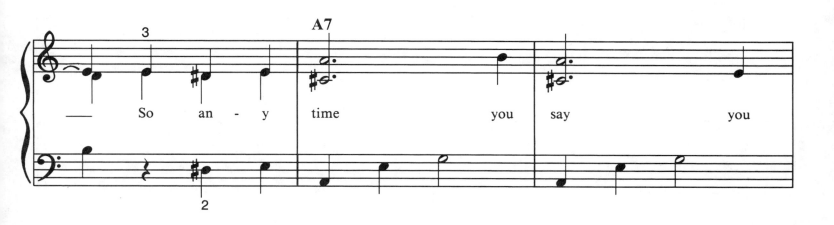

— So an - y time · · · you say · · · you

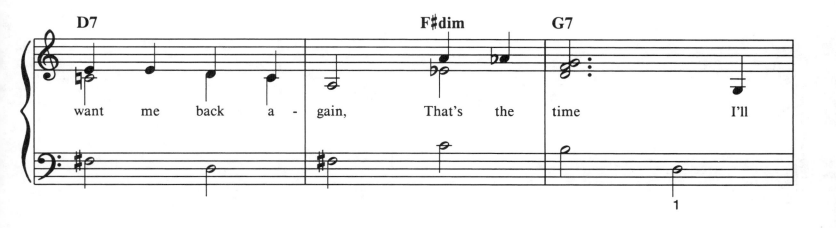

want me back a - gain, That's the time · · · I'll

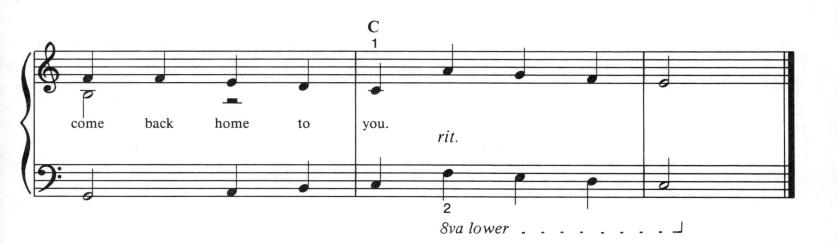

come back home to you. *rit.*

8va lower . . . .

AMONG MY SOUVENIRS

Words by EDGAR LESLIE
Music by HORATIO NICHOLLS

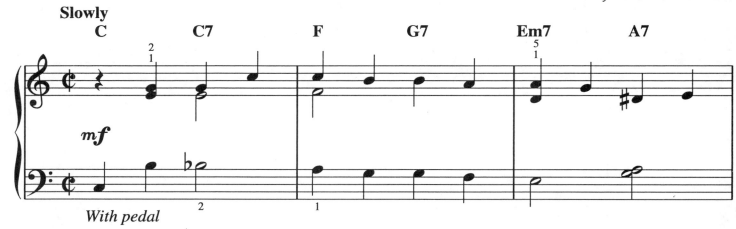

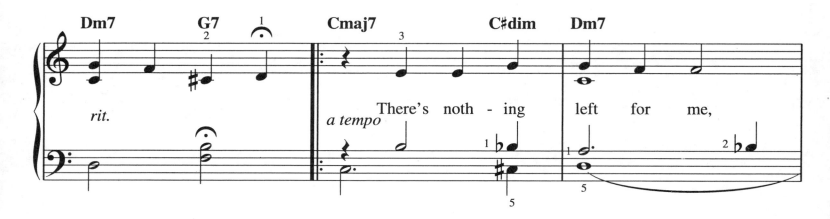

There's noth - ing left for me,

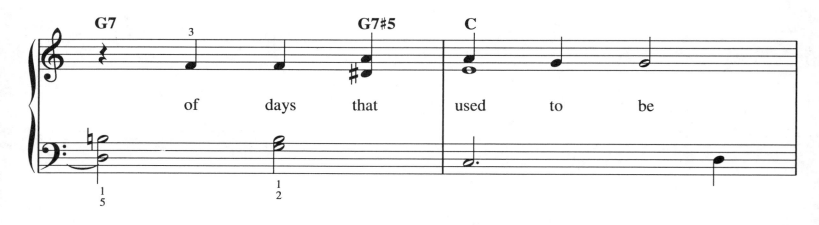

of days that used to be

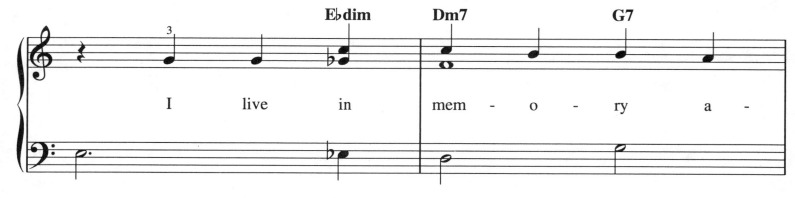

I live in mem - o - ry a -

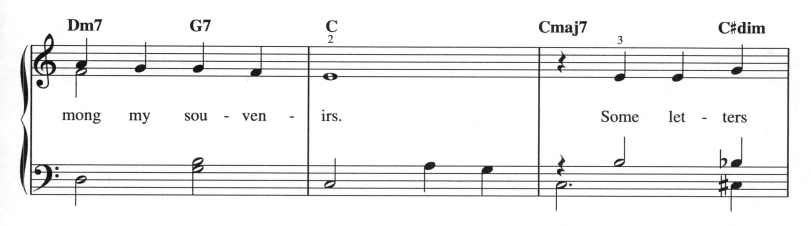

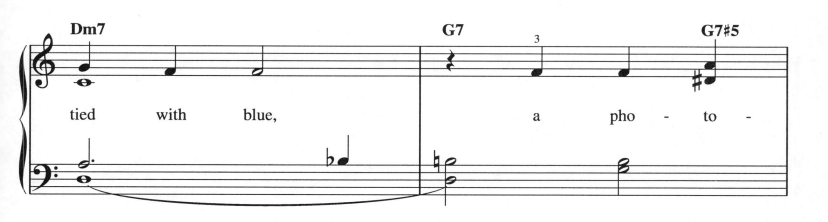

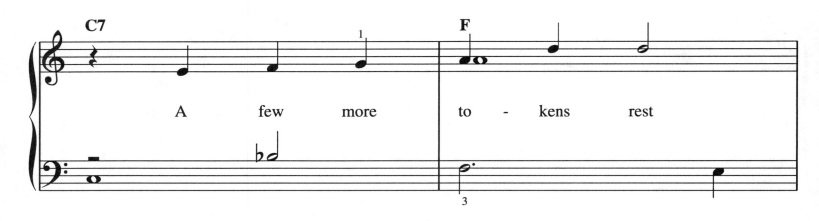

A few more to - kens rest

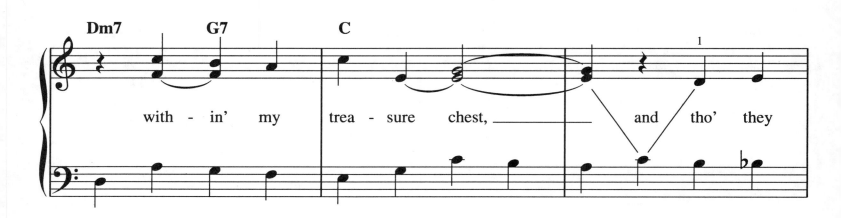

with - in' my trea - sure chest, _____ and tho' they

do their best to give me con - so -

la - tion. I count them all a - part,

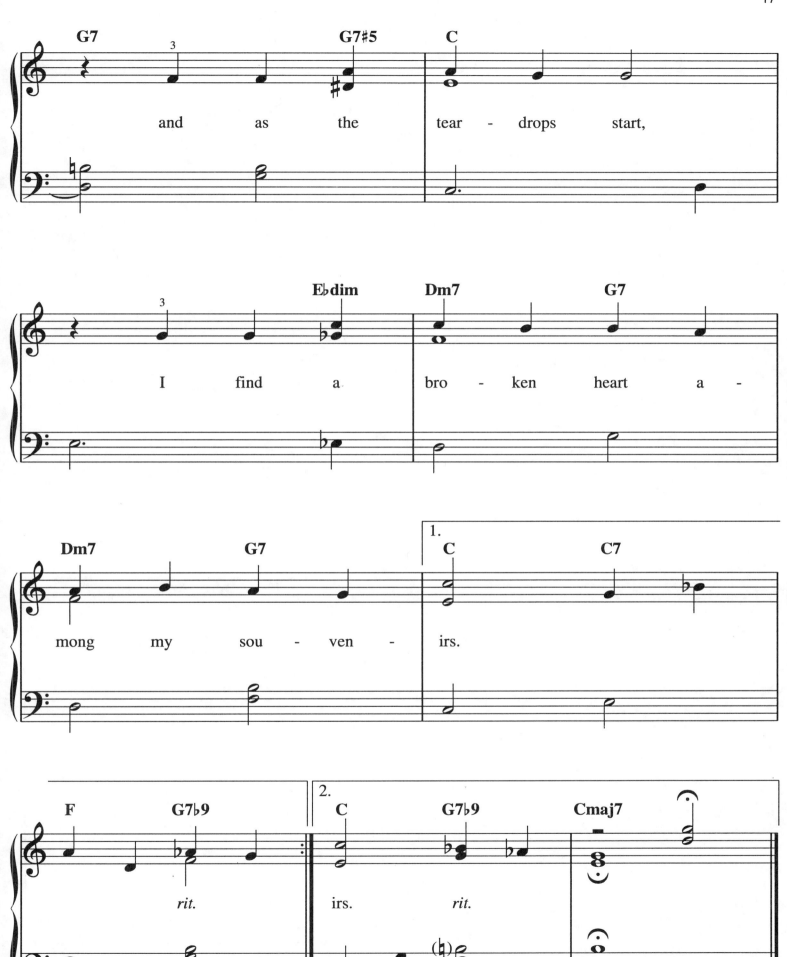

APRIL IN PARIS

Words by E.Y. Harburg
Music by VERNON DUKE

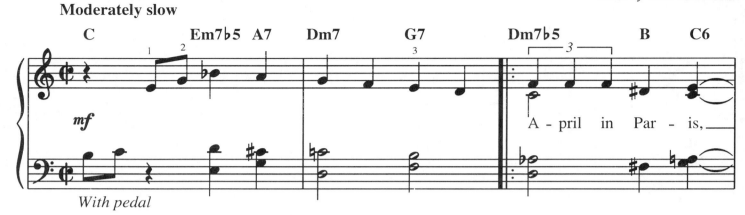

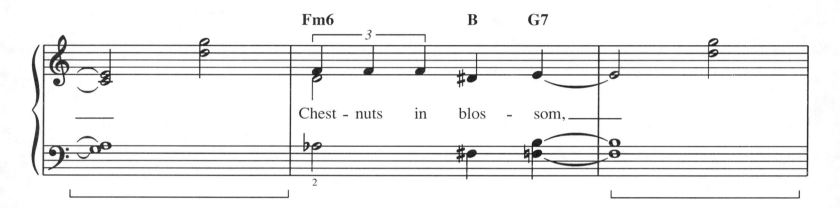

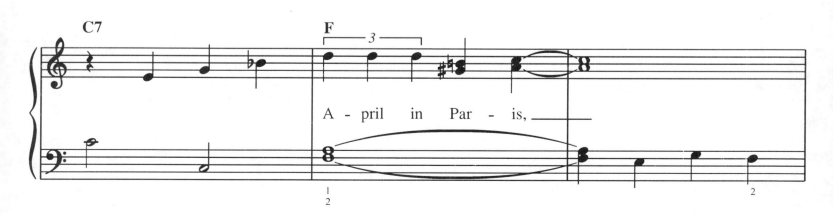

THE BLUE ROOM

from THE GIRL FRIEND

Words by LORENZ HART
Music by RICHARD RODGERS

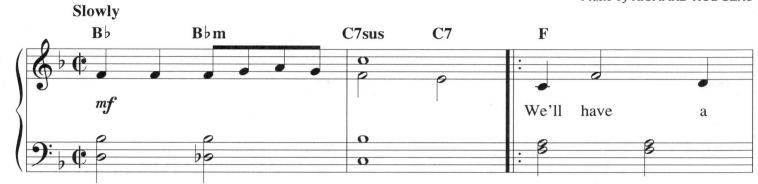

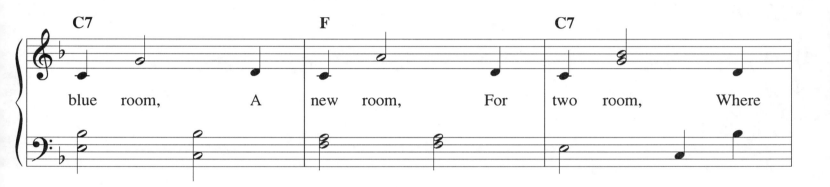

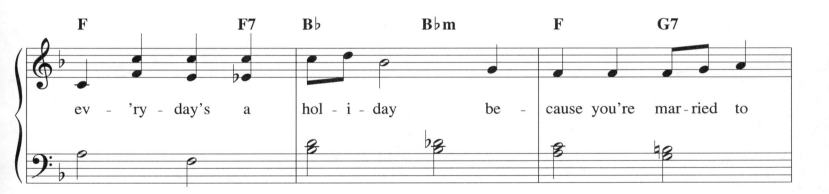

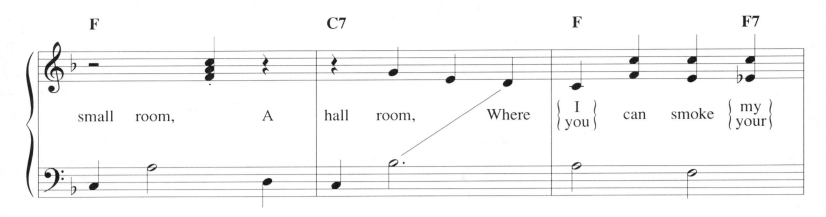

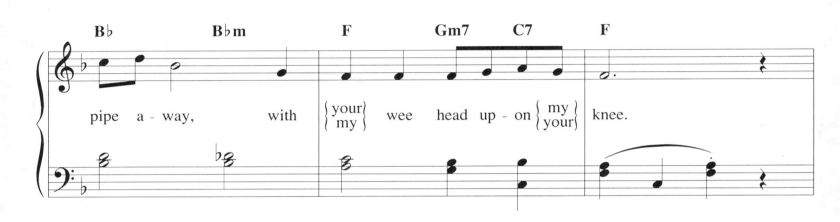

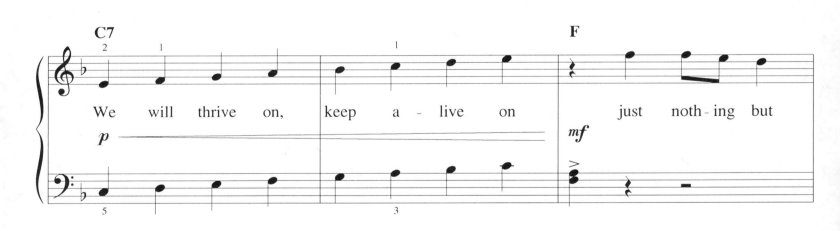

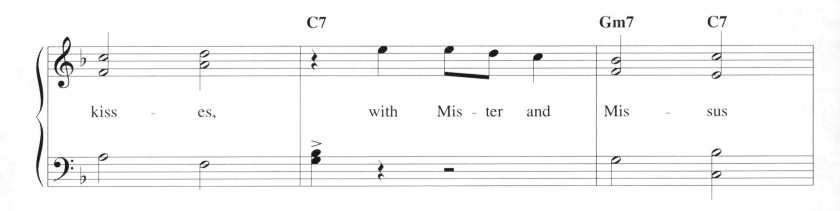

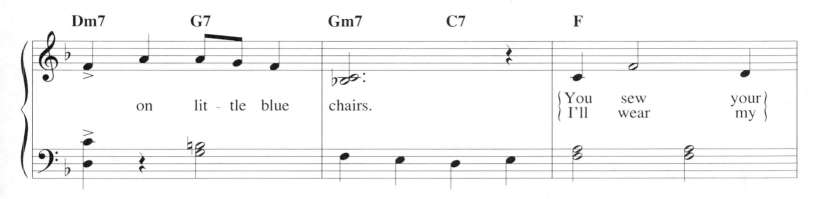

on lit – tle blue chairs. {You sew your} {I'll wear my}

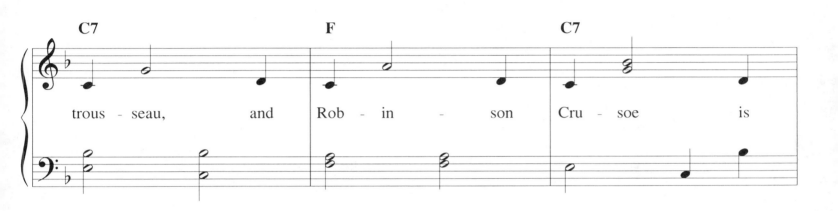

trous – seau, and Rob – in – son Cru – soe is

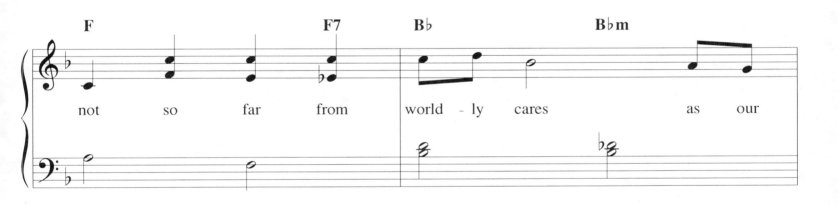

not so far from world – ly cares as our

blue room far a – way up – stairs! stairs!

BILL
from SHOW BOAT

Lyrics by P.G. WODEHOUSE and OSCAR HAMMERSTEIN II
Music by JEROME KERN

25

BODY AND SOUL

Words by EDWARD HEYMAN,
ROBERT SOUR and FRANK EYTON
Music by JOHN GREEN

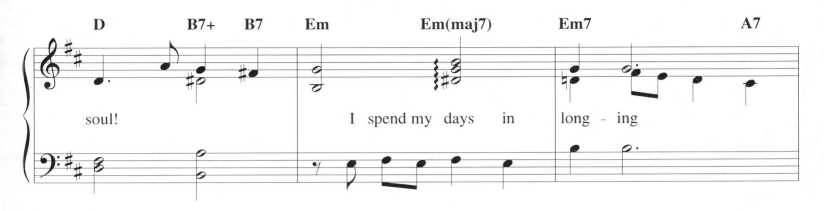

soul! I spend my days in long - ing

and won-d'ring why it's me you're wrong - ing, I tell you I

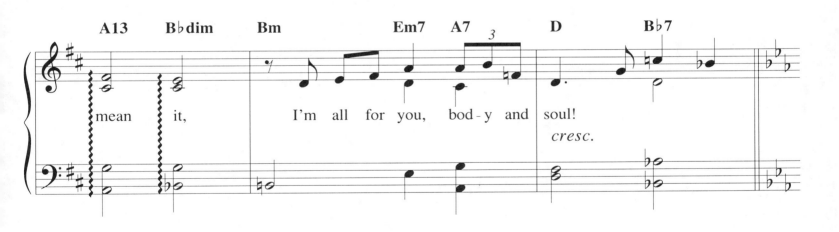

mean it, I'm all for you, bod - y and soul!

cresc.

mf I can't be - lieve it, it's hard to con - ceive it that

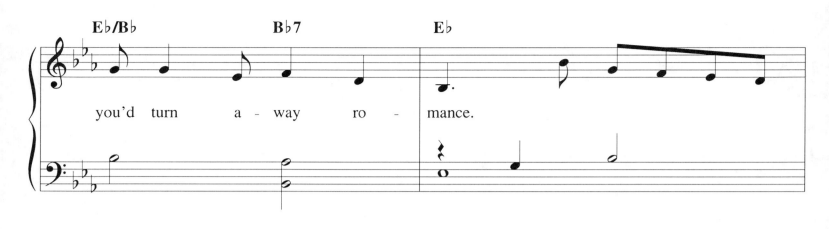

you'd turn a - way ro - mance.

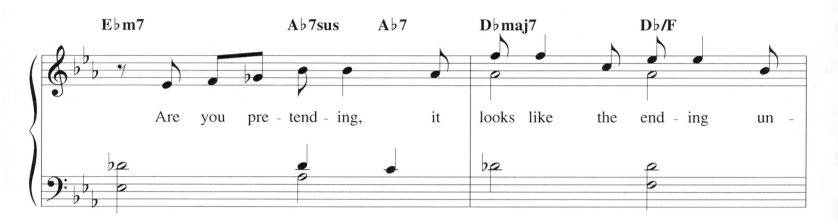

Are you pre - tend - ing, it looks like the end - ing un -

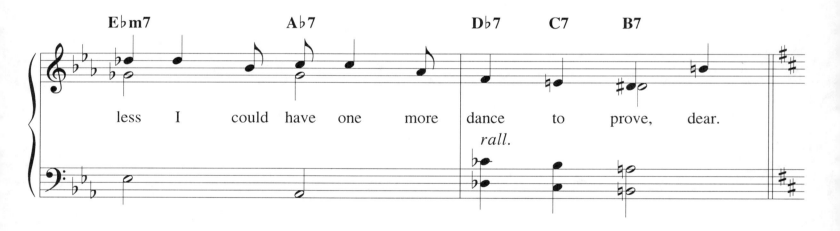

less I could have one more dance to prove, dear.

rall.

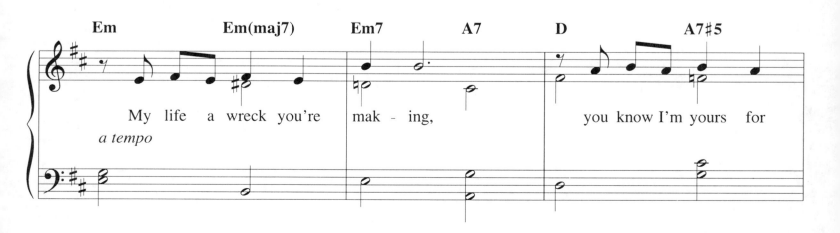

My life a wreck you're mak - ing, you know I'm yours for

a tempo

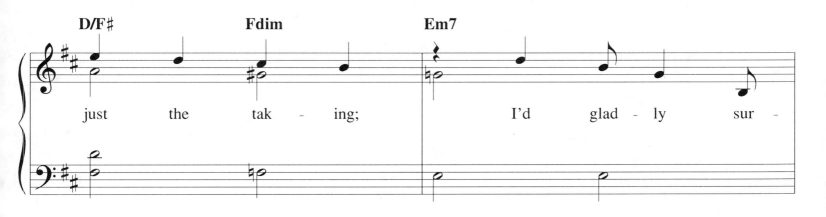

just the tak - ing; I'd glad - ly sur -

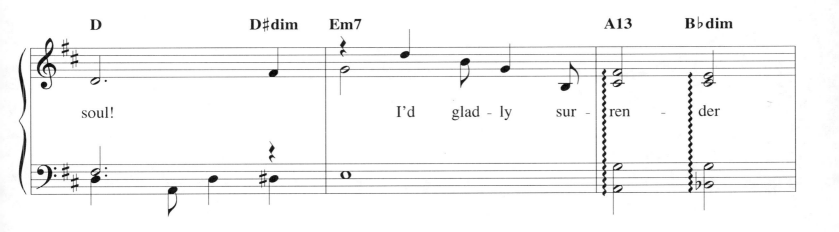

ren - der my - self to you, bod - y and

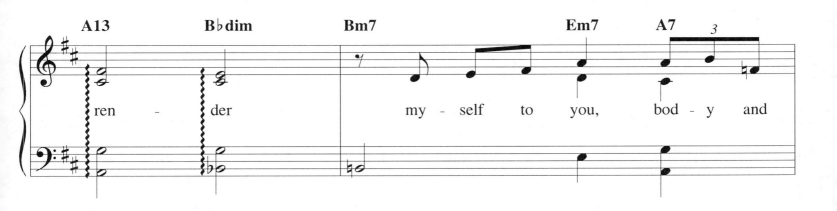

soul! I'd glad - ly sur - ren - der

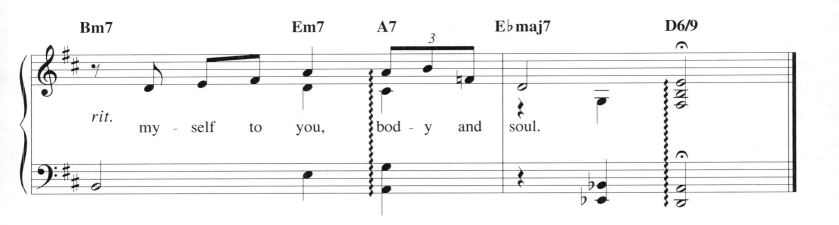

rit. my - self to you, bod - y and soul.

BUTTON UP YOUR OVERCOAT

from FOLLOW THRU
from GOOD NEWS

Words and Music by B.G. DeSYLVA,
LEW BROWN and RAY HENDERSON

But - ton up your o - ver - coat ___
But - ton up your o - ver - coat ___

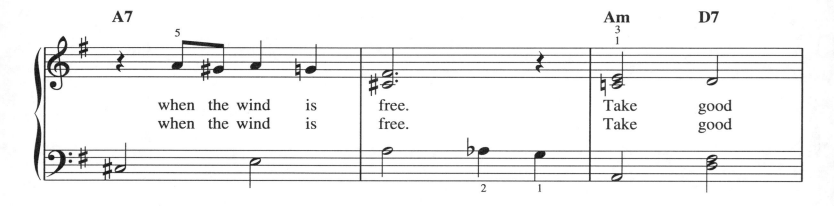

when the wind is free. Take good
when the wind is free. Take good

care of your - self ___ you be - long to me! ___
care of your - self ___ you be - long to me! ___

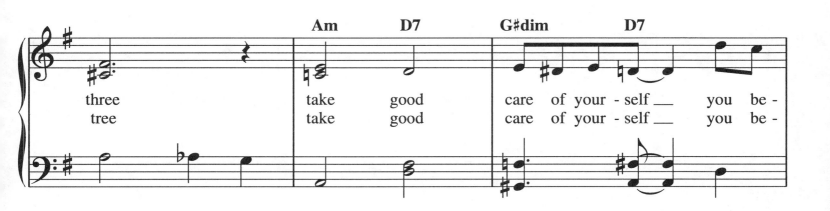

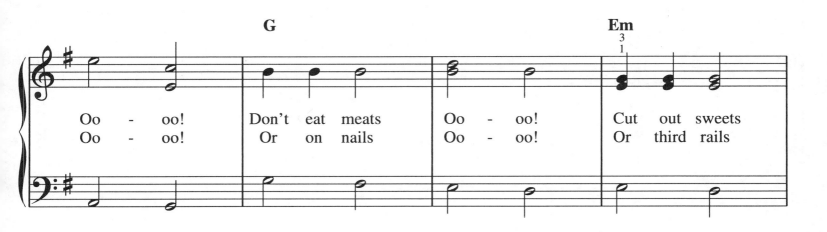

32

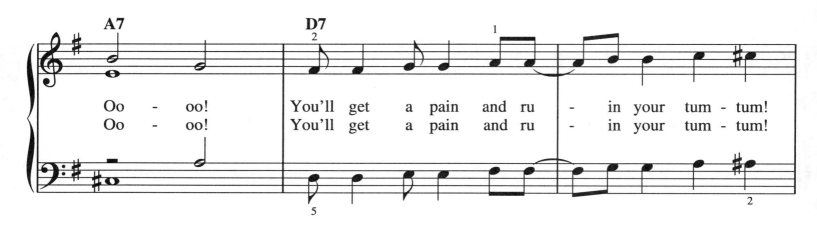

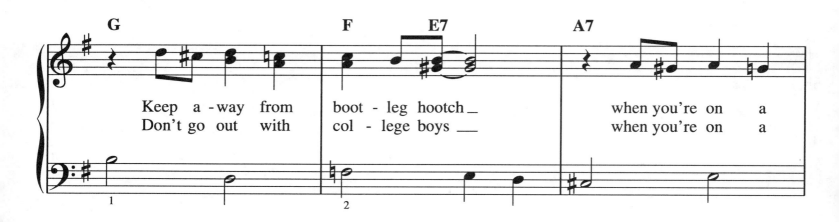

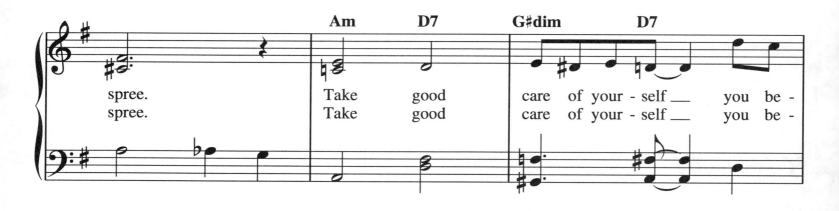

CAN'T HELP LOVIN' DAT MAN

from SHOW BOAT

Lyrics by OSCAR HAMMERSTEIN II
Music by JEROME KERN

Can't help lov-in' dat man— of mine.
getting faster - - - - - - - - - - -

When he goes a - way
a little faster

Dat's a rain-y day, And when he comes

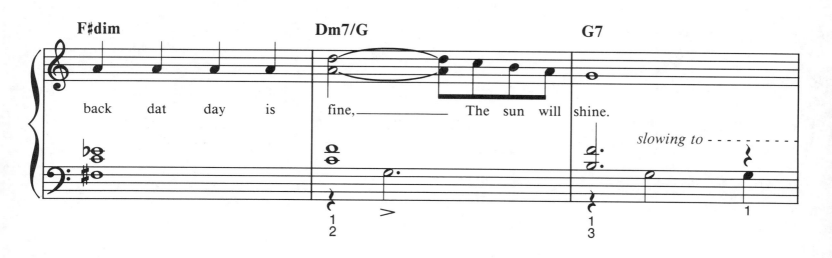

back dat day is fine,——— The sun will shine.
slowing to - - - - - - - -

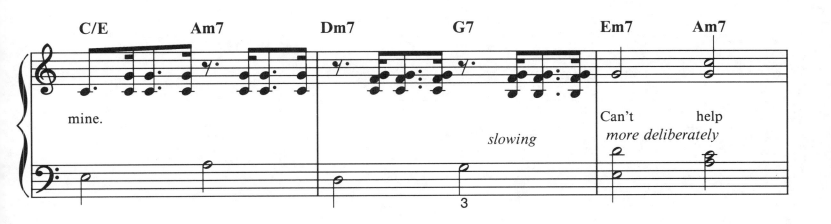

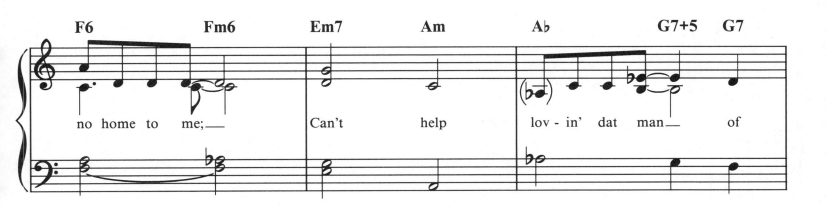

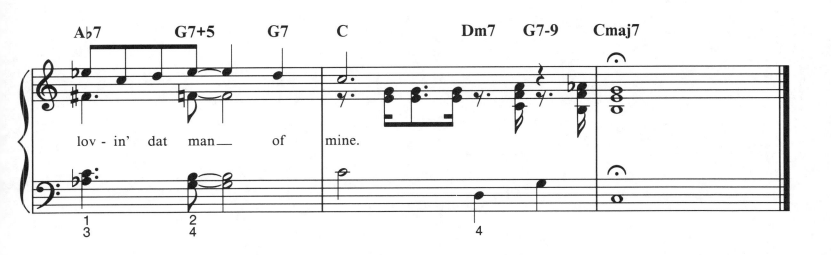

CHEEK TO CHEEK
from the RKO Radio Motion Picture TOP HAT

Words and Music by
IRVING BERLIN

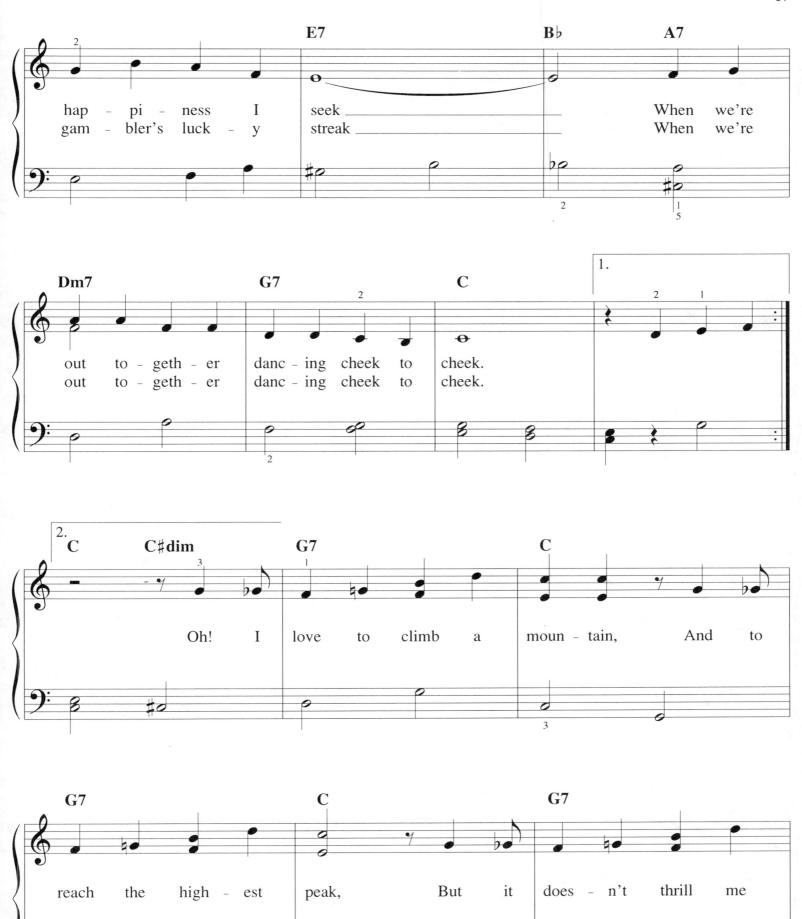

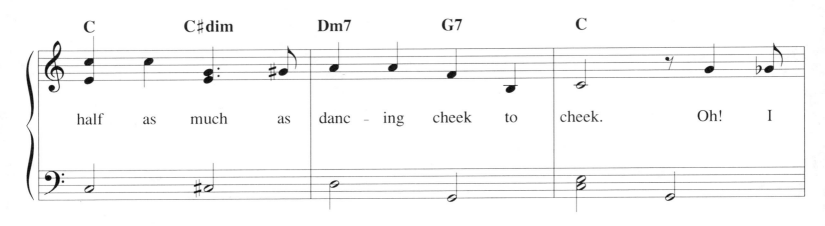

half as much as danc - ing cheek to cheek. Oh! I

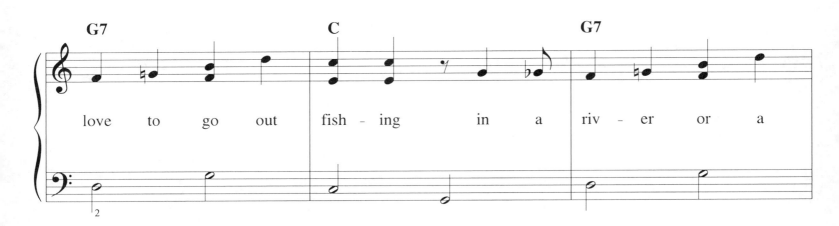

love to go out fish - ing in a riv - er or a

creek, But I don't en - joy it half as much As

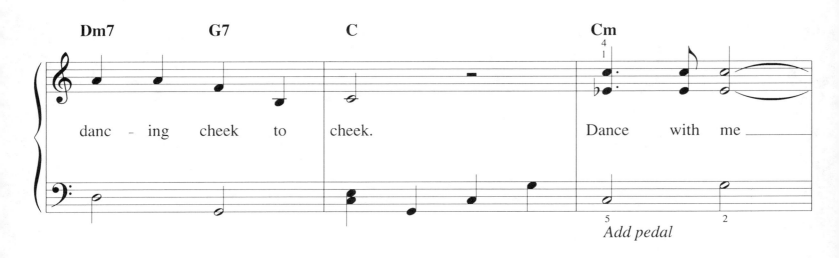

danc - ing cheek to cheek. Dance with me ___

Add pedal

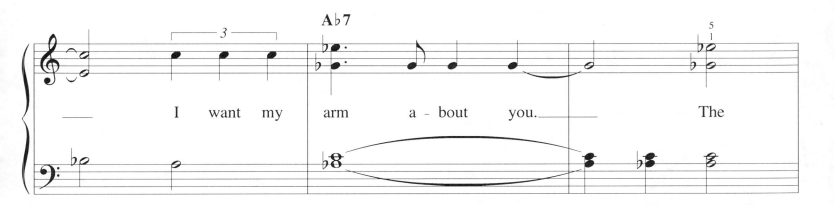

I want my arm a - bout you.___ The

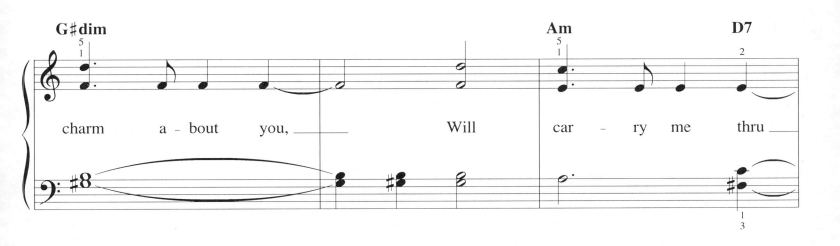

charm a - bout you,___ Will car - ry me thru___

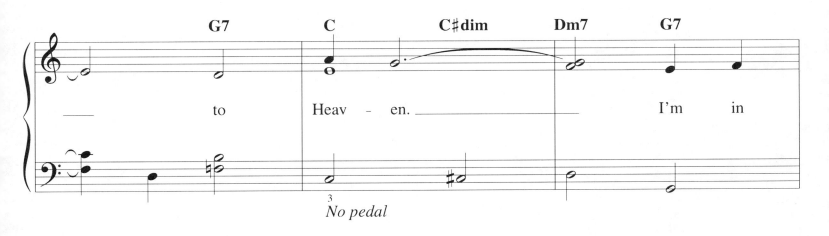

___ to Heav - en.___ I'm in

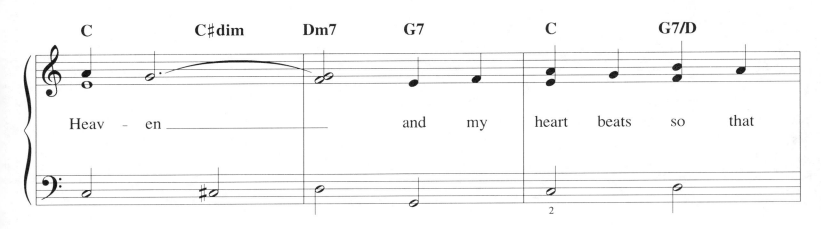

Heav - en ___ and my heart beats so that

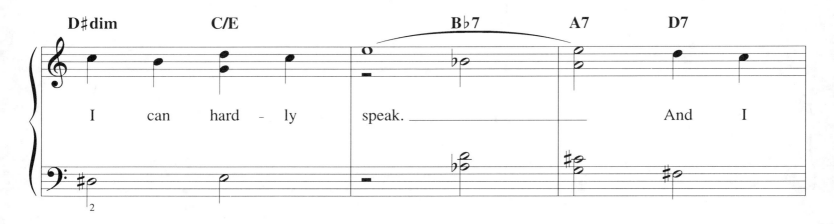

I can hard - ly speak. _____ And I

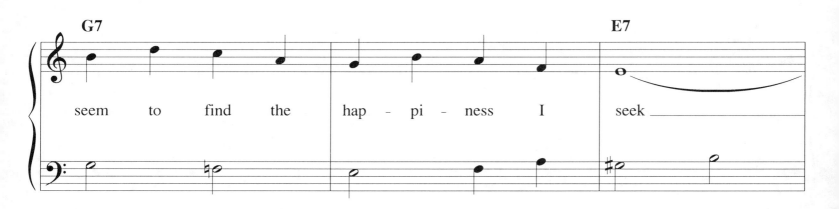

seem to find the hap - pi - ness I seek _____

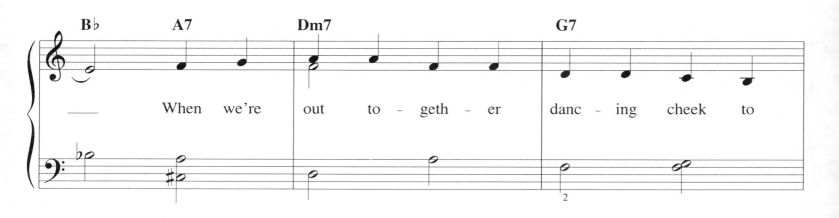

_____ When we're out to - geth - er danc - ing cheek to

cheek. _____

THE GLORY OF LOVE

Words and Music by
BILLY HILL

THE FOLKS WHO LIVE ON THE HILL

from HIGH, WIDE AND HANDSOME

Lyrics by OSCAR HAMMERSTEIN II
Music by JEROME KERN

Some - day ____ we'll build a home on a hill top high, you and I, Shin - y and new a cot - tage that two can fill. ____ And we'll be pleased to be

called _____ "The folks who live on the hill." _____

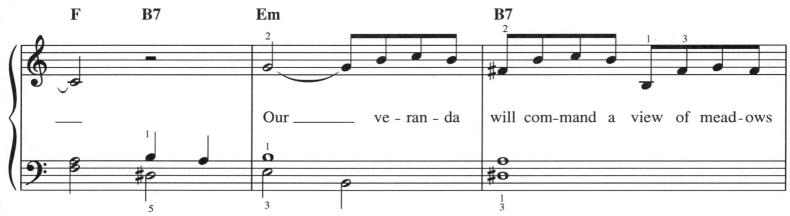

_____ Our _____ ve-ran-da will com-mand a view of mead-ows

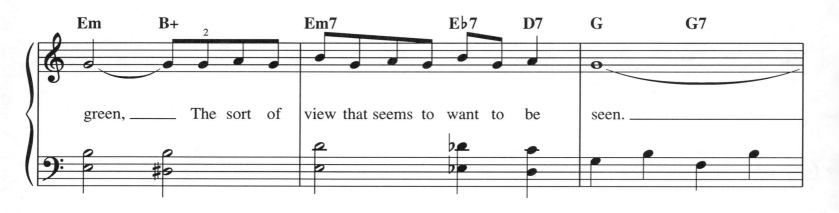

green, _____ The sort of view that seems to want to be seen. _____

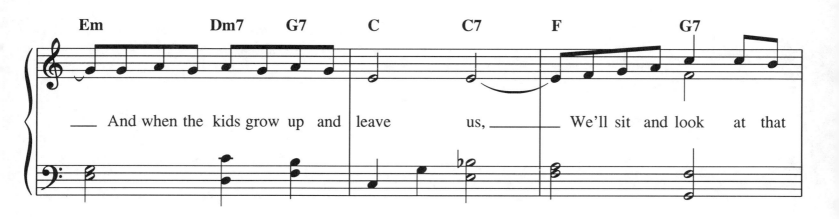

_____ And when the kids grow up and leave us, _____ We'll sit and look at that

THE HAWAIIAN WEDDING SONG
(Ke Kali Nei Au)

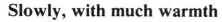

English Lyrics by AL HOFFMAN and DICK MANNING
Hawaiian Lyrics and Music by CHARLES E. KING

Slowly, with much warmth

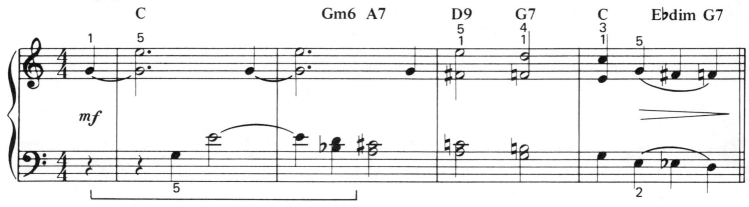

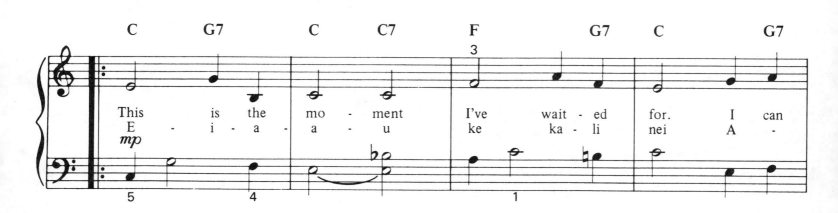

This is the mo - ment I've wait - ed for. I can
E - i - a - a - u ke ka - li nei A -

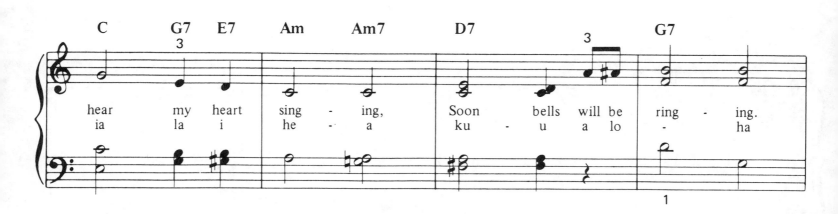

hear my heart sing - ing, Soon bells will be ring - ing.
ia la i he - a ku - u a lo - ha

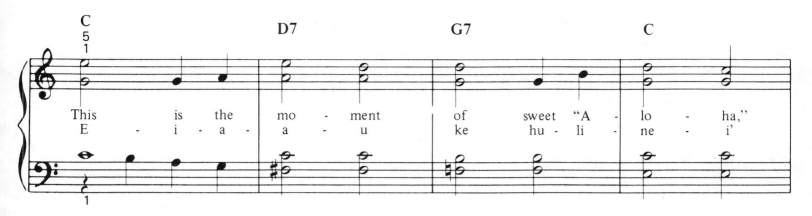

This   is   the   mo - ment   of   sweet "A - lo - ha,"
E   i - a -   a -   u   ke   hu - li - ne - i'

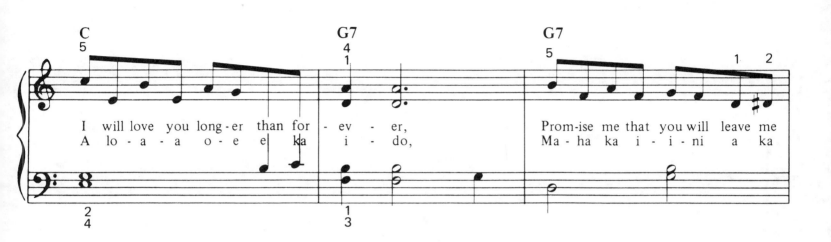

I   will   love   you   long - er   than   for - ev - er,
A   lo - a - a   o - e   e   ka   i - do,

Prom - ise   me   that   you   will   leave   me
Ma - ha   ka   i - i - ni   a   ka

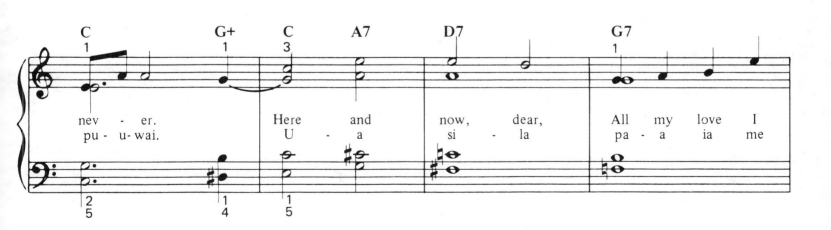

nev - er.   Here   and   now,   dear,   All   my   love   I
pu - u - wai.   U -   a   si - la   pa - a   ia   me

vow,   dear.   Prom - ise   me   that   you   will   leave   me   nev - er,
o -   e   Ko   a   lo   ha   ma   ka   mae   e   i   po

I will love you long-er than for - ev - er.
Ka - iu ia e le - i a - e ne - i la

Now that we are
Nou no ka i -

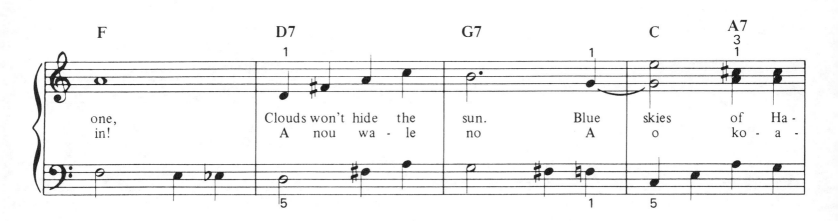

one,
in!

Clouds won't hide the
A nou wa - le

sun.
no

Blue
A

skies
o

of Ha -
ko - a -

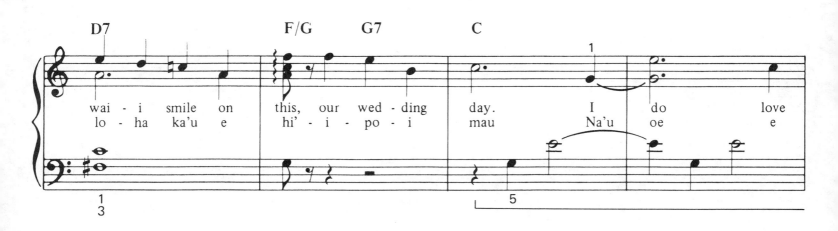

wai - i smile on
lo - ha ka'u e

this, our wed - ding
hi' - i - po - i

day.
mau

I
Na'u

do
oe

love
e

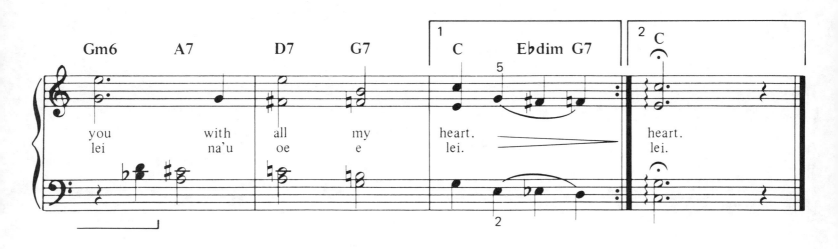

you
lei

with
na'u

all
oe

my
e

heart.
lei.

heart.
lei.

HOW ABOUT ME?

Words and Music by
IRVING BERLIN

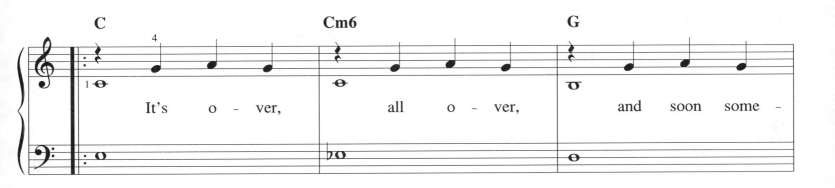

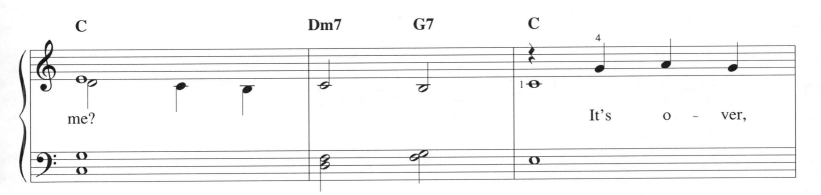

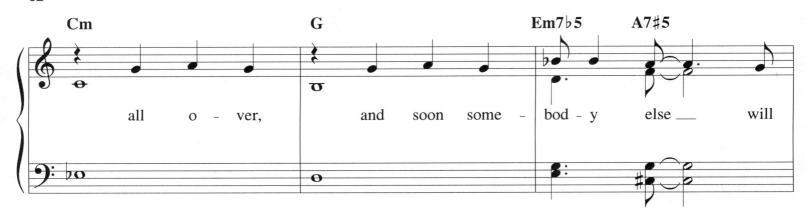

all o - ver, and soon some - bod - y else ___ will

tell his friends ___ a - bout you. But how ___ a - bout me?

You'll find some - bod - y new. ___ But what am

I to do? ___ I'll still re - mem - ber you ___

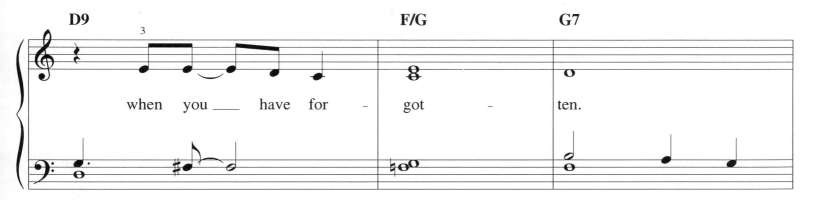

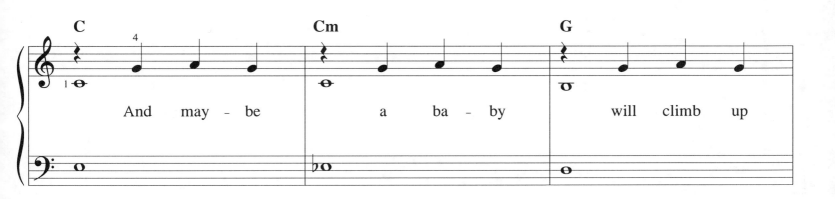

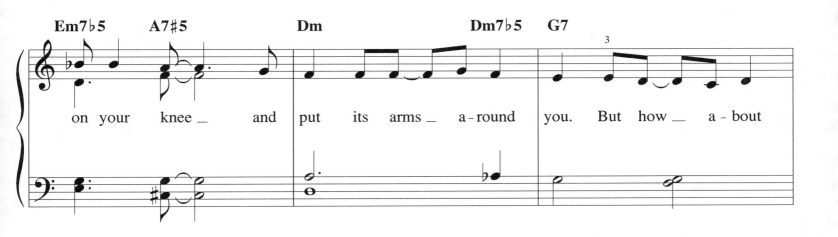

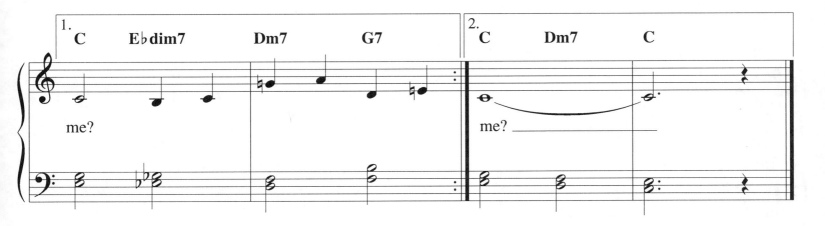

HEART AND SOUL

from the Paramount Short Subject A SONG IS BORN

Words by FRANK LOESSER
Music by HOAGY CARMICHAEL

Moderately, not too fast

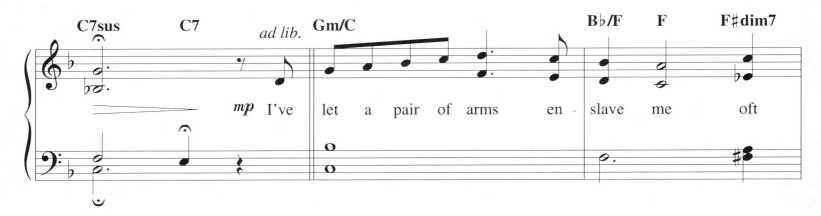

I've let a pair of arms en-slave me oft

times be - fore, but more than just a thrill you

gave me, yes more, much more.

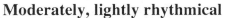

Moderately, lightly rhythmical

Heart and soul, ____ I fell in love with you. Heart and soul,

the way a fool would do, mad - ly, be-cause you held me

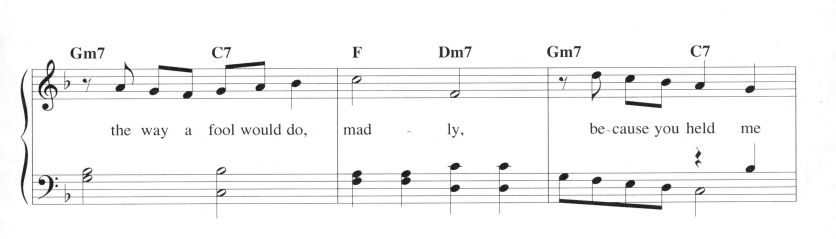

tight and stole a kiss in the night. Heart and soul, ____

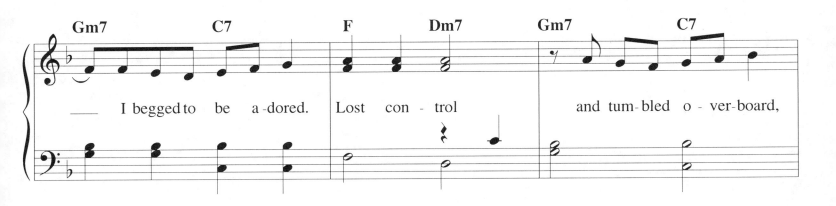

____ I begged to be a-dored. Lost con - trol and tum-bled o - ver-board,

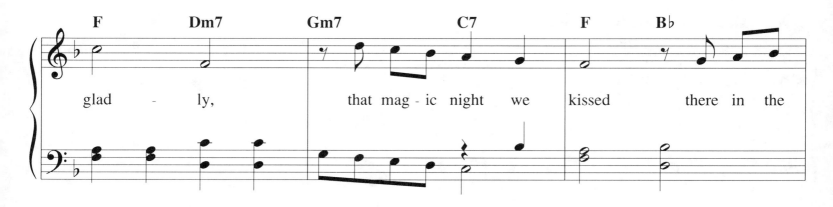

glad - ly, that mag - ic night we kissed there in the

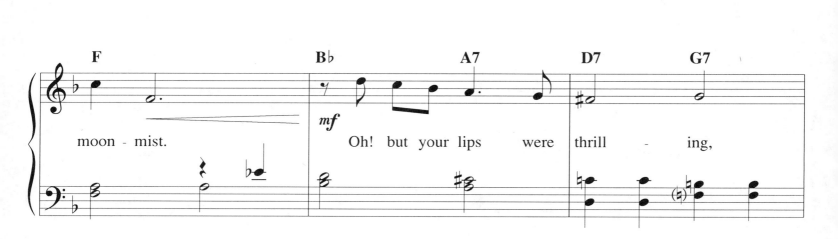

moon - mist. Oh! but your lips were thrill - ing,

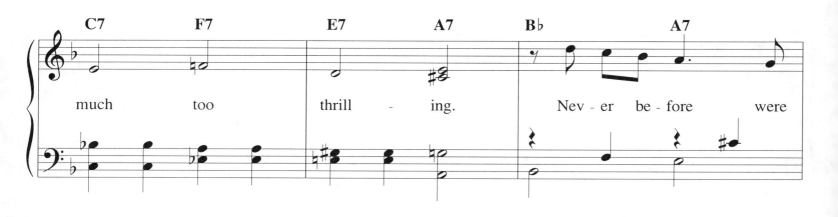

much too thrill - ing. Nev - er be - fore were

mine so strange - ly will - ing. But

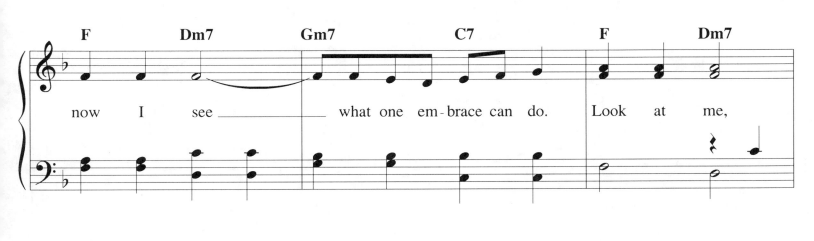

now I see _____ what one em-brace can do. Look at me,

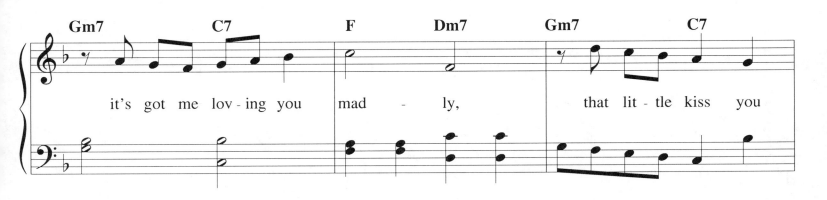

it's got me lov-ing you mad — ly, that lit-tle kiss you

1.

stole held all my heart and soul.

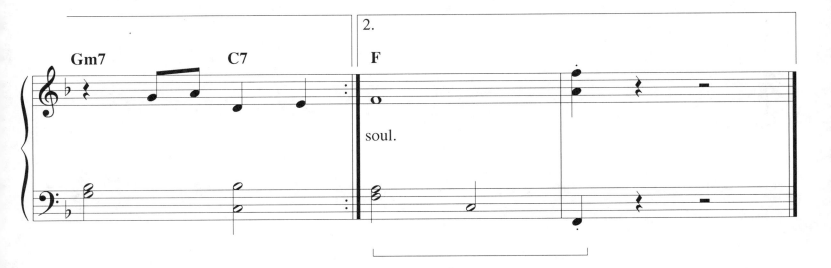

2.

soul.

HONEYSUCKLE ROSE
from AIN'T MISBEHAVIN'

Words by ANDY RAZAF
Music by THOMAS "FATS" WALLER

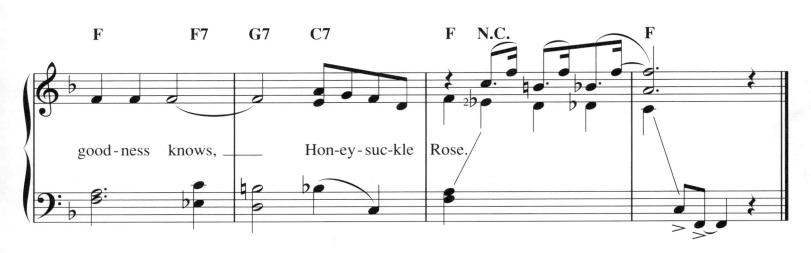

HOW DEEP IS THE OCEAN
(How High Is the Sky)

Words and Music by
IRVING BERLIN

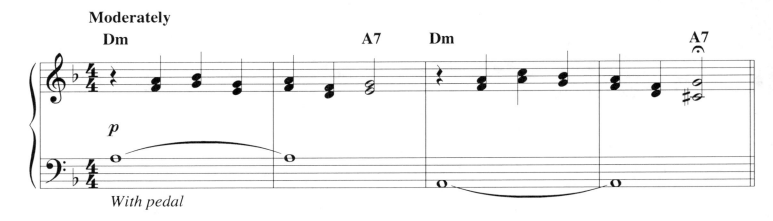

With pedal

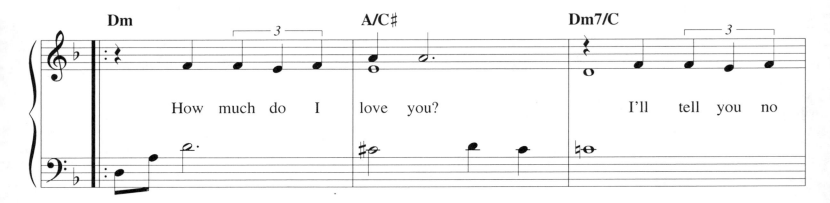

How much do I love you? I'll tell you no

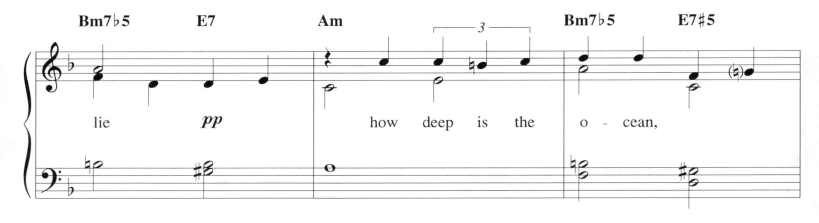

lie   *pp*   how deep is the o - cean,

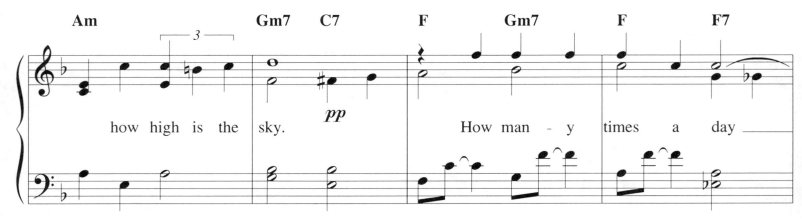

how high is the sky.   *pp*   How man-y times a day ___

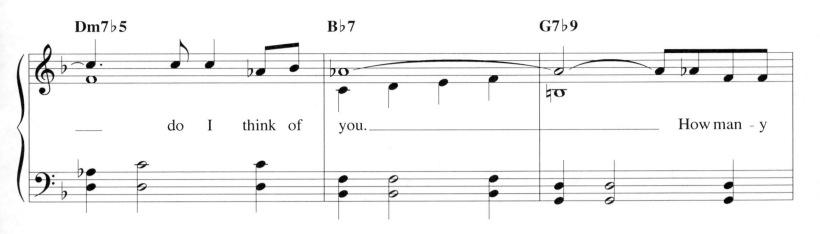

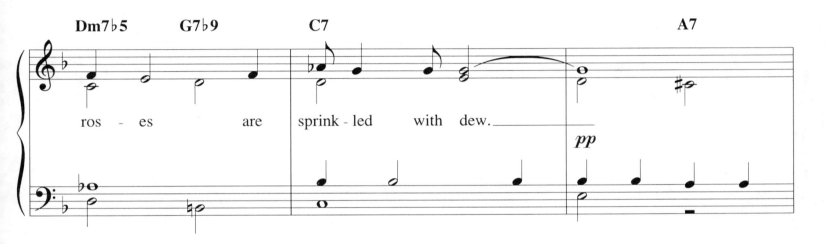

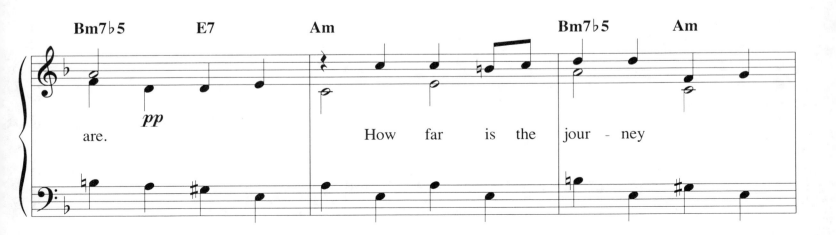

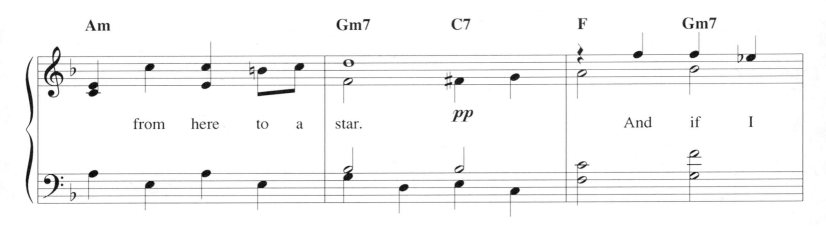

from here to a star. *pp* And if I

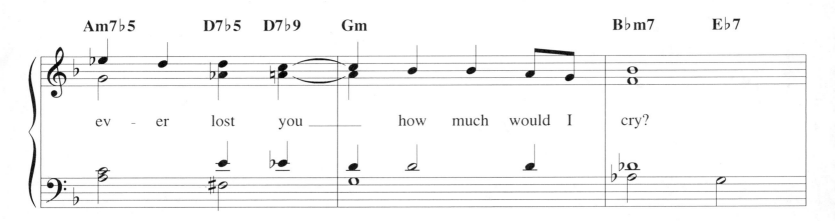

ev - er lost you _____ how much would I cry?

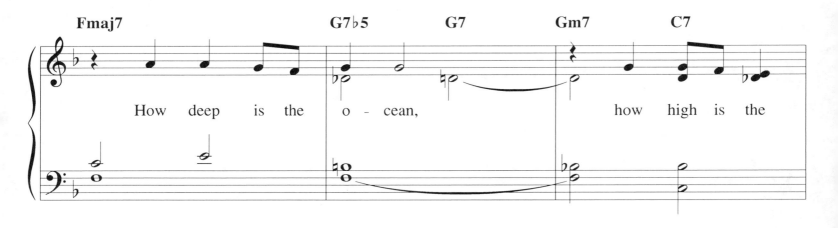

How deep is the o - cean, how high is the

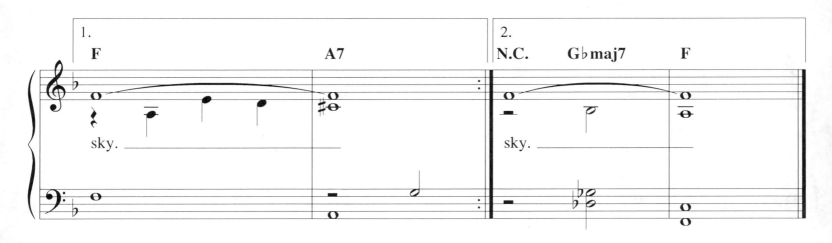

sky. _____ sky. _____

I CAN'T GIVE YOU ANYTHING BUT LOVE

from BLACKBIRDS OF 1928

Words by DOROTHY FIELDS
Music by JIMMY McHUGH

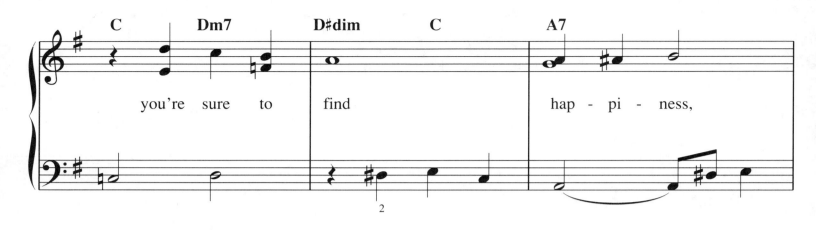

you're sure to find | hap - pi - ness,

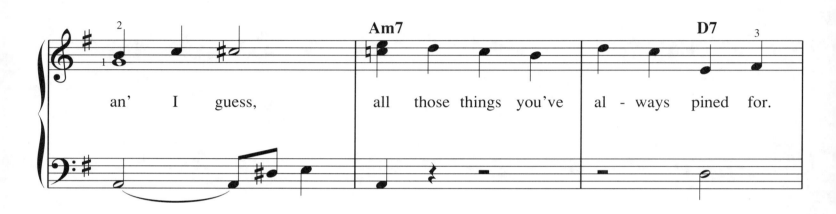

an' I guess, | all those things you've | al - ways pined for.

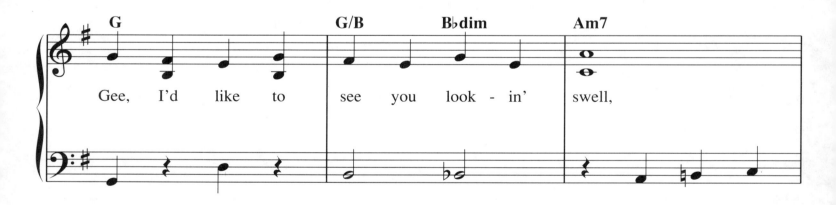

Gee, I'd like to | see you look - in' | swell,

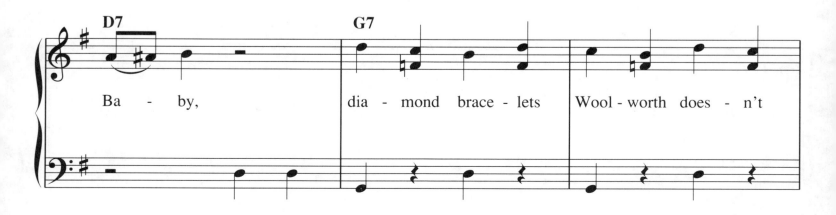

Ba - by, | dia - mond brace - lets | Wool - worth does - n't

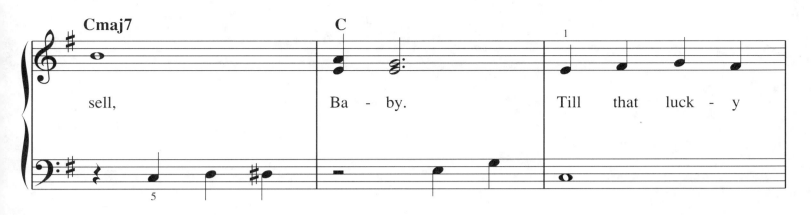

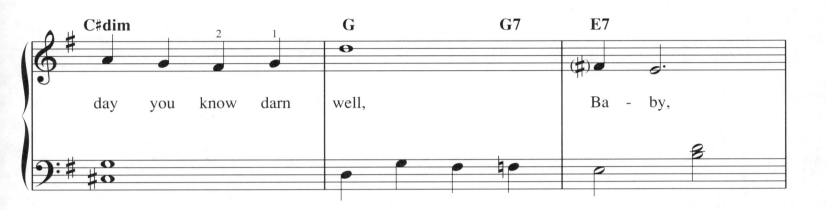

I'VE GOT MY LOVE TO KEEP ME WARM

from the 20th Century Fox Motion Picture ON THE AVENUE

Words and Music by
IRVING BERLIN

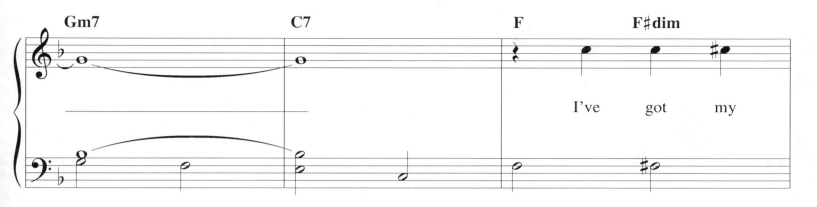

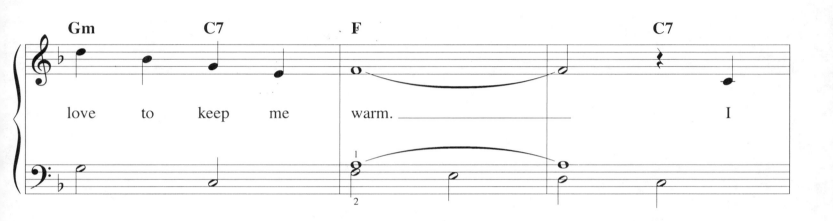

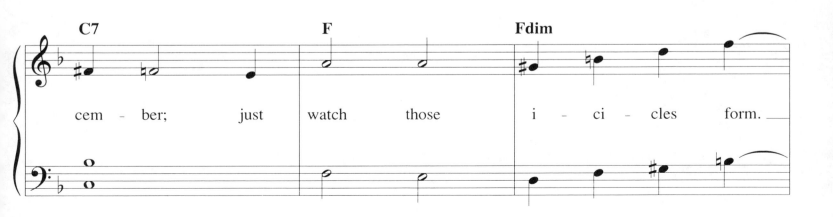

What do I care if

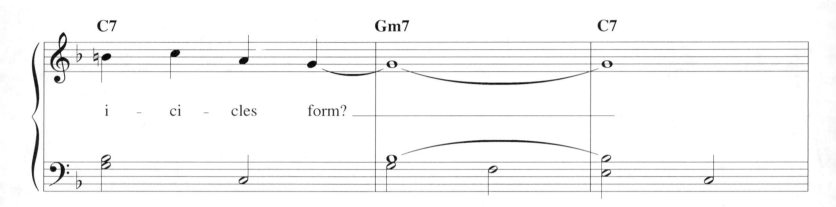

i - ci - cles form?

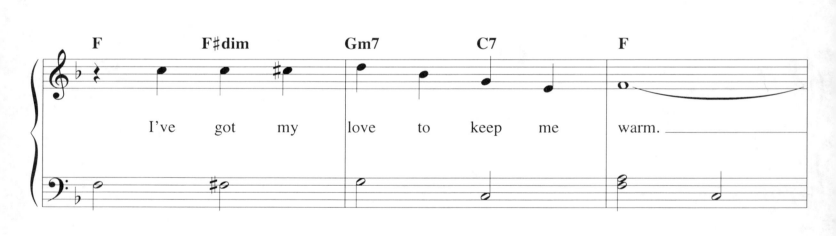

I've got my love to keep me warm.

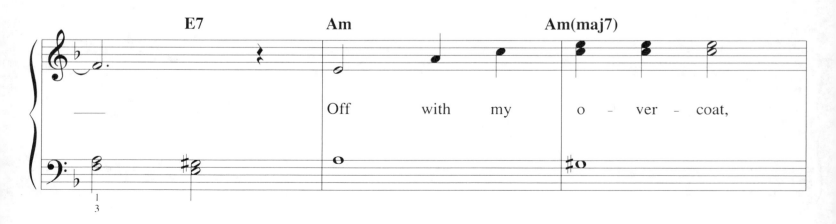

Off with my o - ver - coat,

off with my glove. I need no

o – ver – coat, I'm burn –ing with love. My

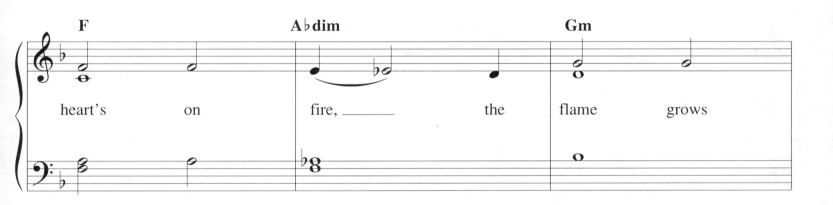

heart's on fire, _____ the flame grows

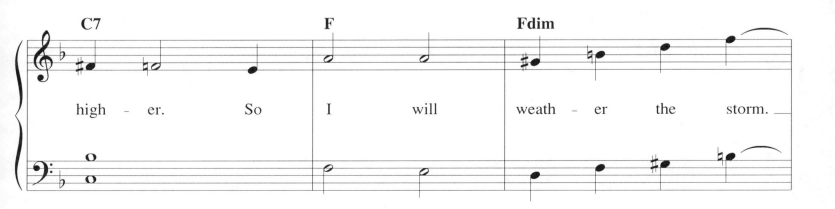

high – er. So I will weath – er the storm.

Gm7

What do I care how

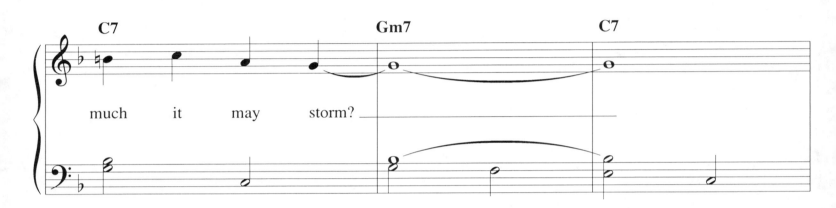

C7   **Gm7**   **C7**

much   it   may   storm? _____

F   **F♯dim**   **Gm7**   **C7**   **1.** **F**

I've   got   my   love   to   keep   me   warm. _____

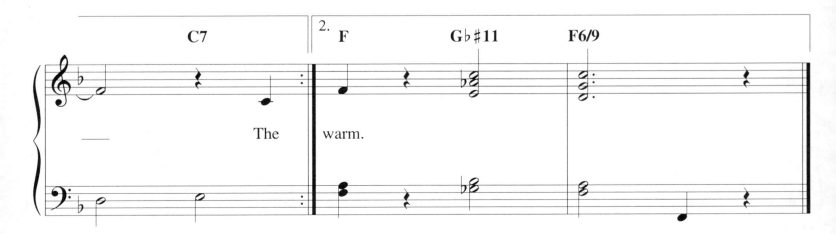

C7   **2.** **F**   **G♭♯11**   **F6/9**

_____   The   warm.

I'VE GOT YOU UNDER MY SKIN

from BORN TO DANCE

Words and Music by
COLE PORTER

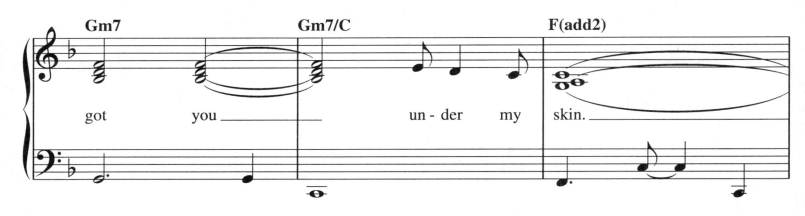

got you _____ un - der my skin. _____

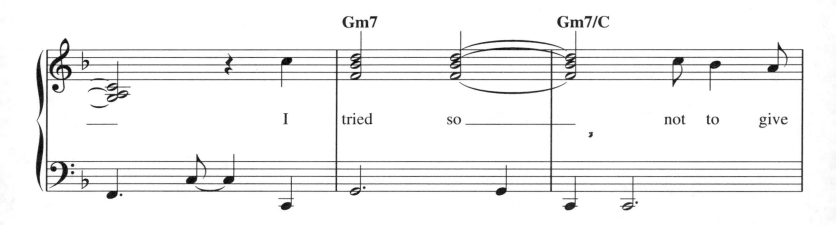

_____ I tried so _____ not to give

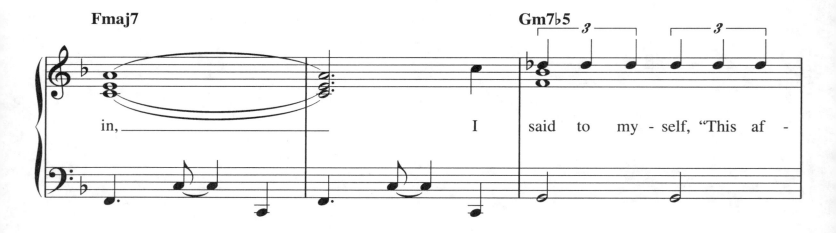

in, _____ I said to my - self, "This af -

fair nev - er will go so well." _____ But

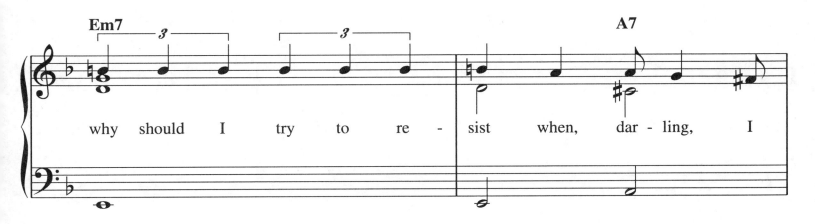

why should I try to re - sist when, dar - ling, I

know so well ____ I've got you ____

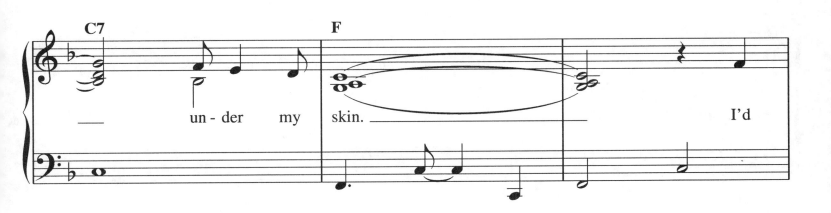

____ un - der my skin. ____ I'd

sac - ri - fice an - y - thing, Come what might, for the

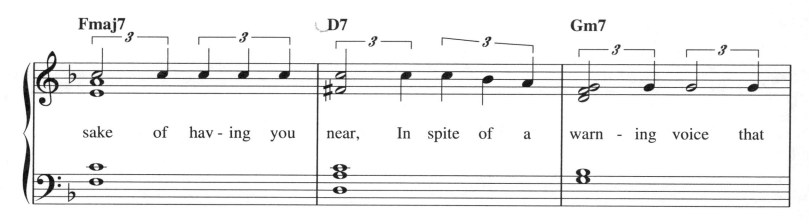

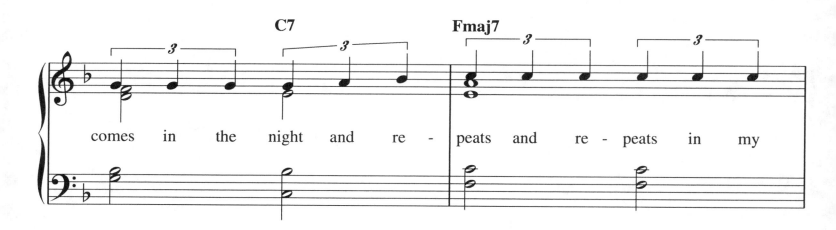

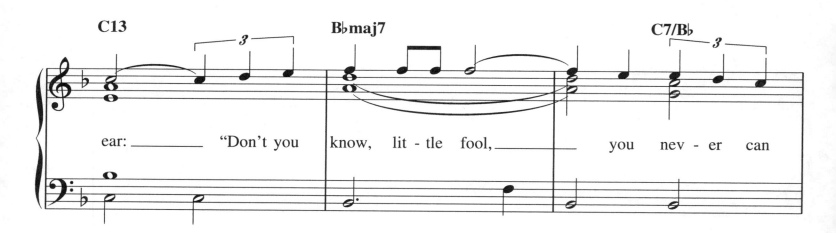

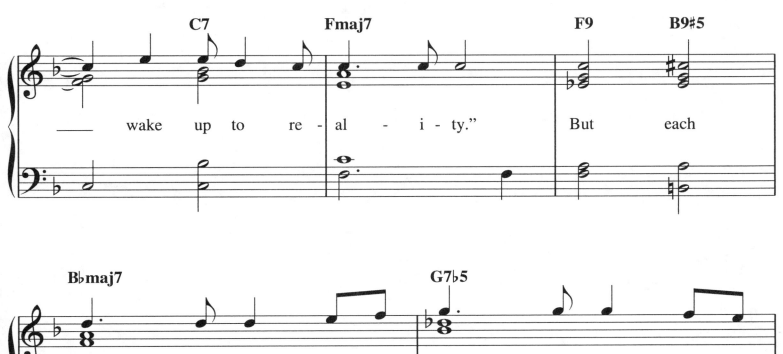

_____ wake up to re - al - i - ty." But each

time I do, just the thought of you makes me

stop, Be - fore I be - gin, 'cause I've got you _____

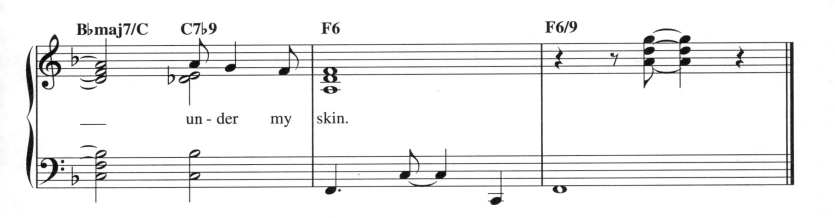

_____ un - der my skin.

IN A SENTIMENTAL MOOD

Words and Music by DUKE ELLINGTON,
IRVING MILLS and MANNY KURTZ

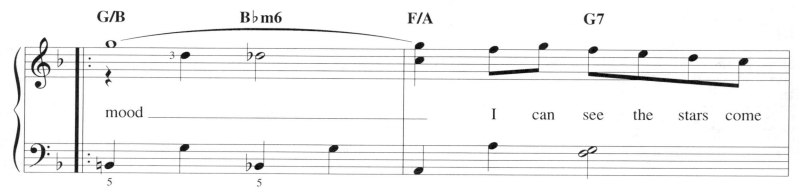

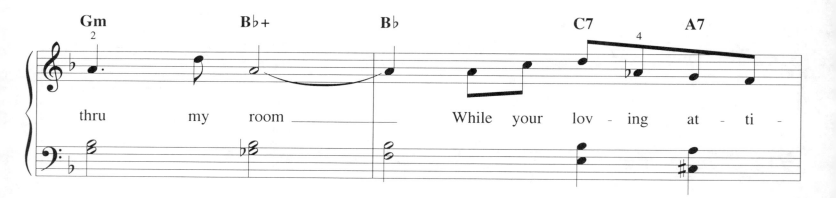

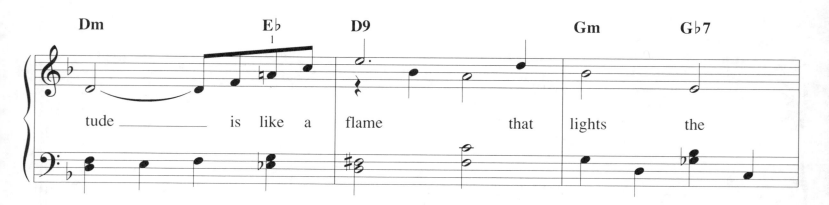

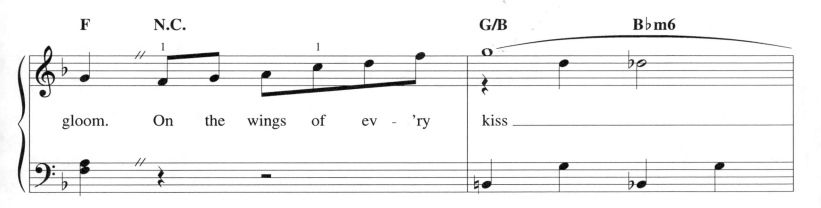

gloom.   On   the   wings   of   ev - ʼry   kiss _____

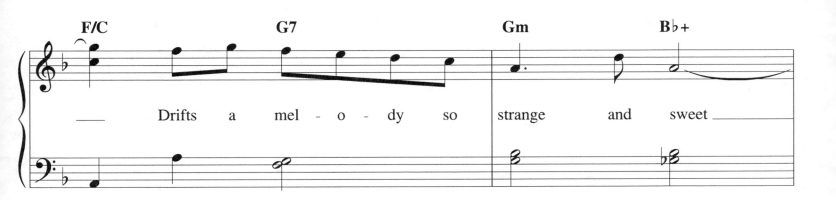

_____   Drifts   a   mel - o - dy   so   strange   and   sweet _____

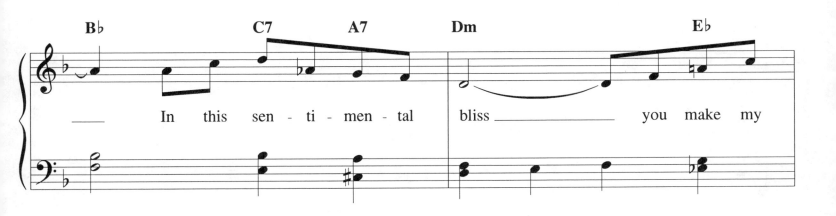

_____   In   this   sen - ti - men - tal   bliss _____   you   make   my

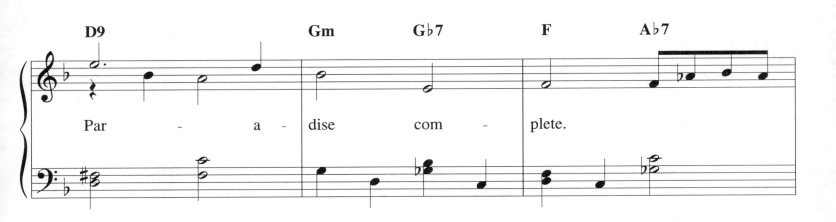

Par - a - dise   com - plete.

78

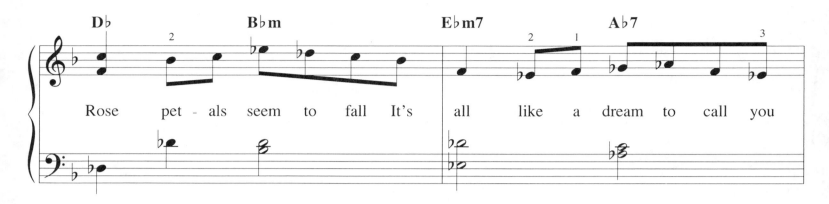

Rose pet - als seem to fall It's all like a dream to call you

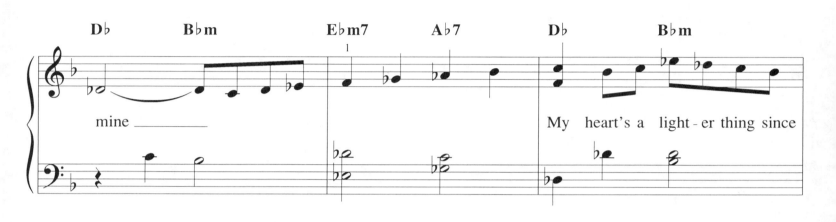

mine _____ My heart's a light - er thing since

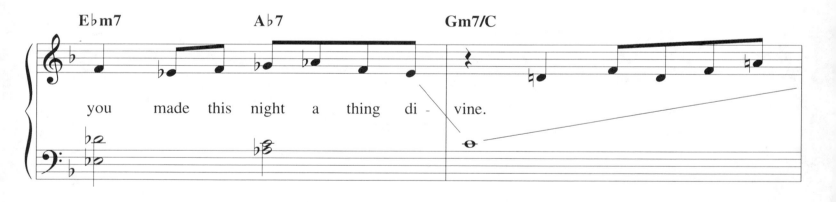

you made this night a thing di - vine.

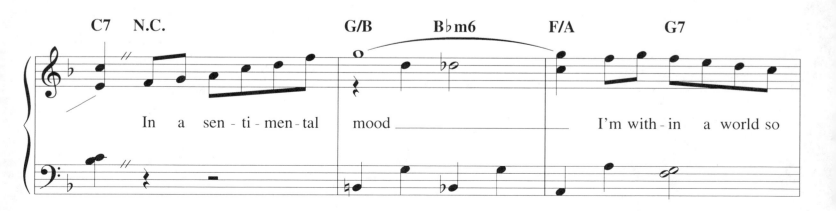

In a sen - ti - men - tal mood _____ I'm with - in a world so

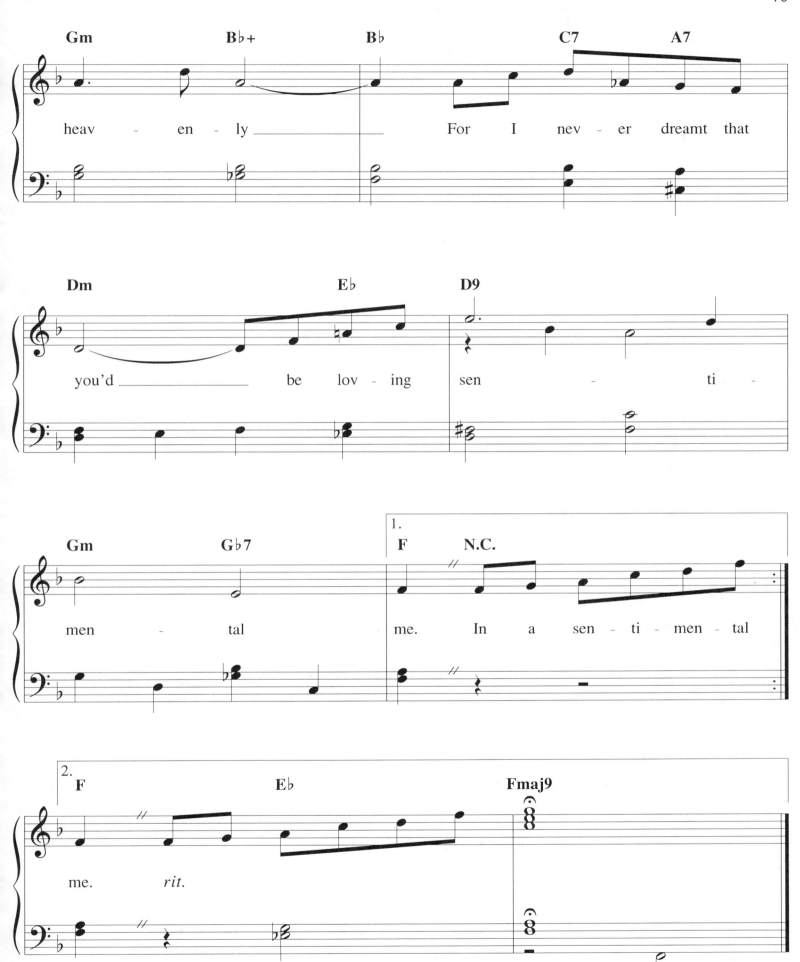

ISN'T IT ROMANTIC?

from the Paramount Picture LOVE ME TONIGHT

Words by LORENZ HART
Music by RICHARD RODGERS

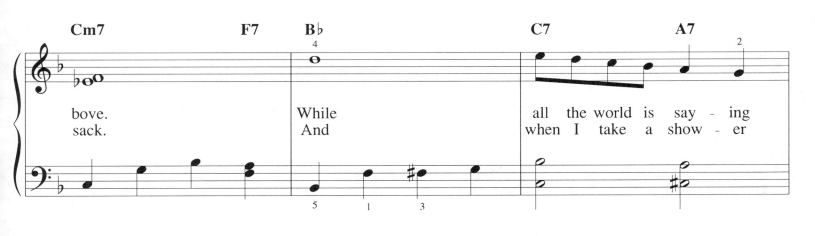

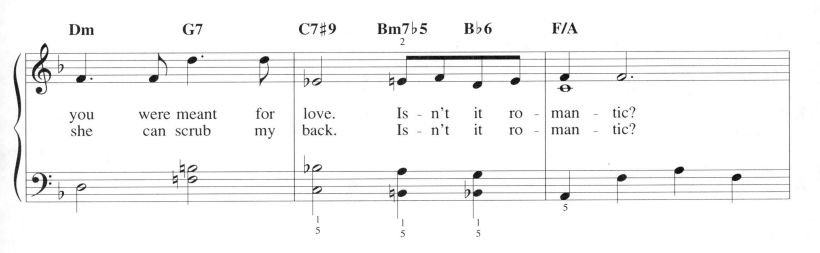

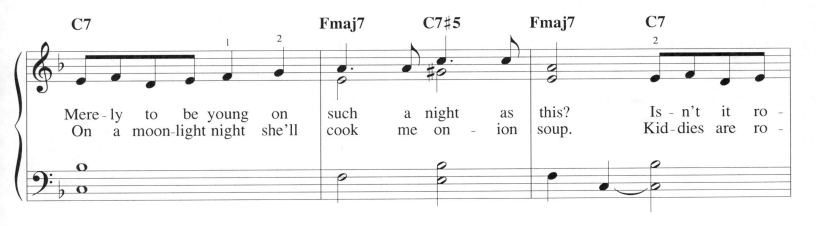

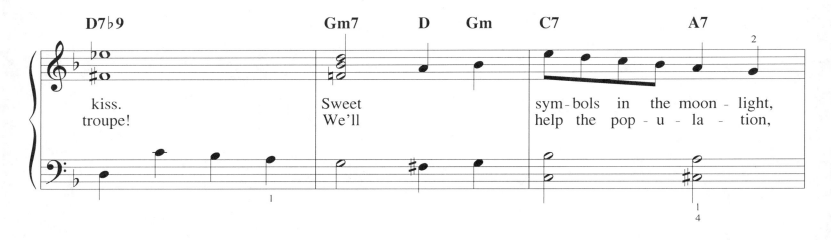

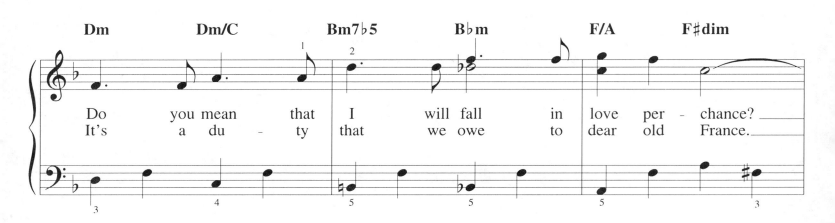

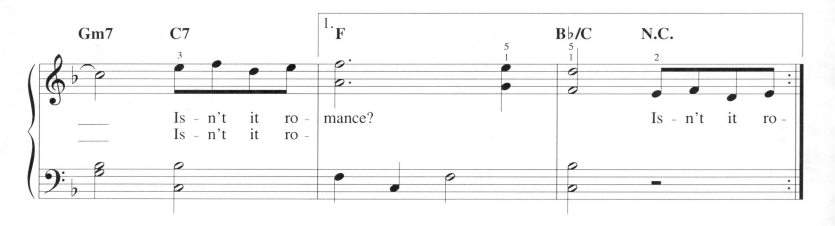

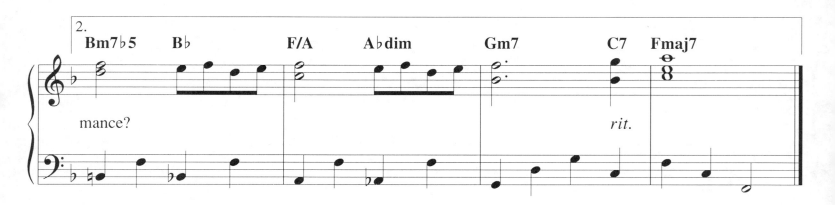

IT'S EASY TO REMEMBER

from the Paramount Picture MISSISSIPPI

Words by LORENZ HART
Music by RICHARD RODGERS

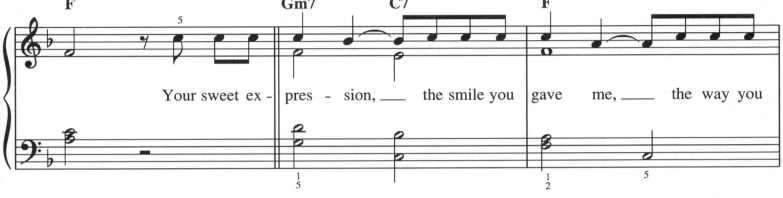

Your sweet ex - pres - sion, ___ the smile you gave me, ___ the way you

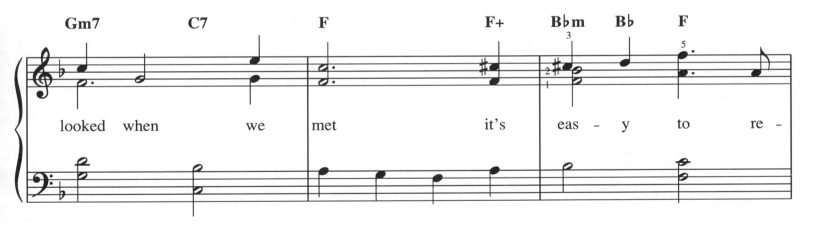

looked when we met it's eas - y to re -

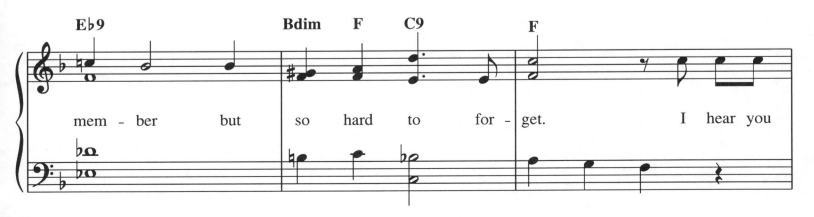

mem - ber but so hard to for - get. I hear you

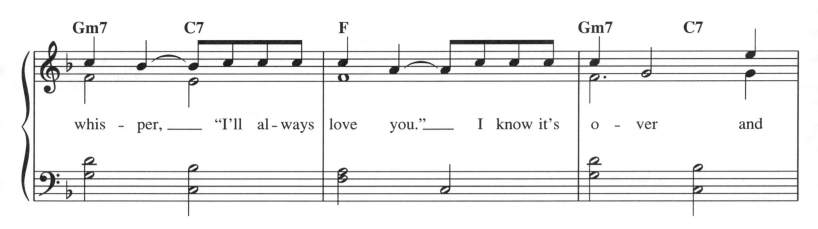

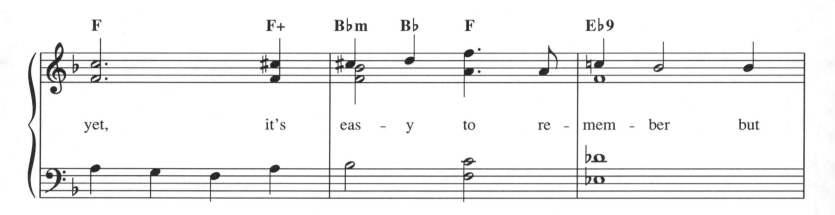

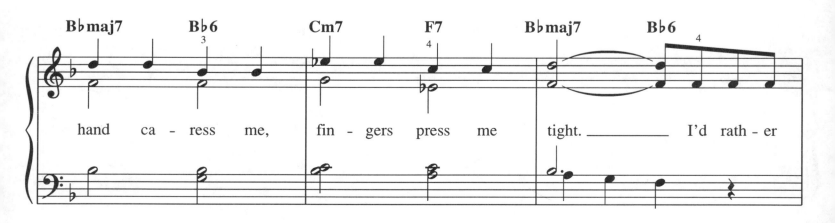

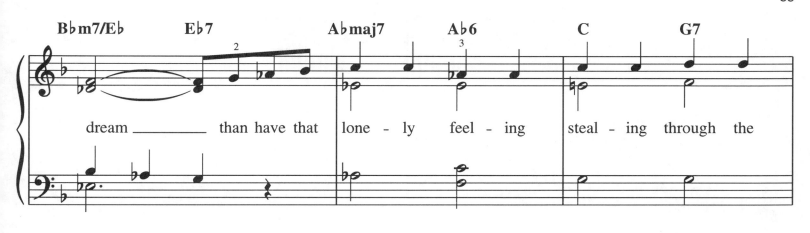

dream _____ than have that | lone - ly feel - ing | steal - ing through the

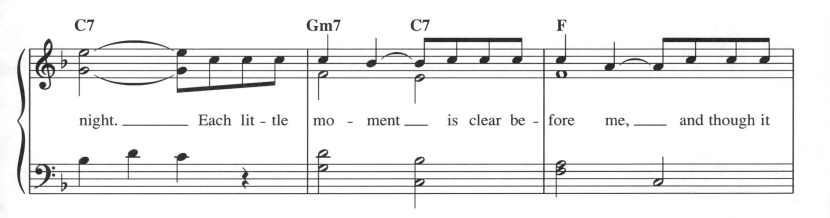

night. _____ Each lit - tle | mo - ment ___ is clear be - fore | me, ___ and though it

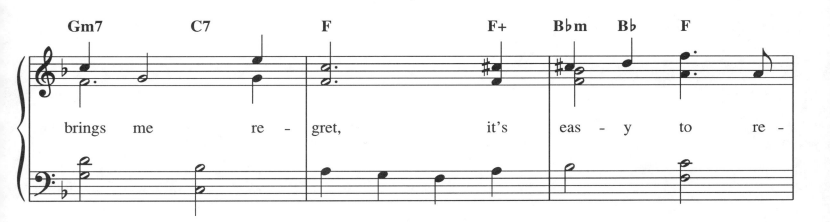

brings me re - | gret, | it's eas - y to re -

mem - ber and | so hard to for - get.

JUNE IN JANUARY
from the Paramount Picture HERE IS MY HEART

Words and Music by LEO ROBIN
and RALPH RAINGER

Moderately slow

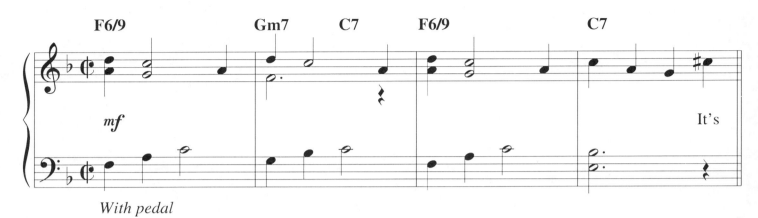

With pedal

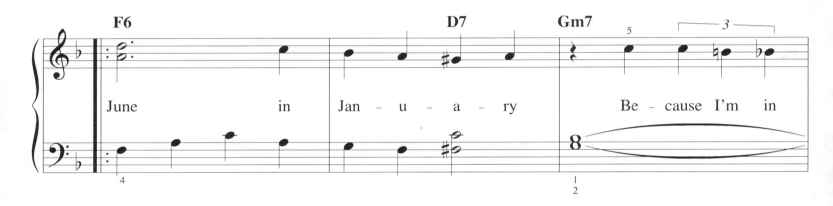

June in Jan-u-a-ry Be-cause I'm in

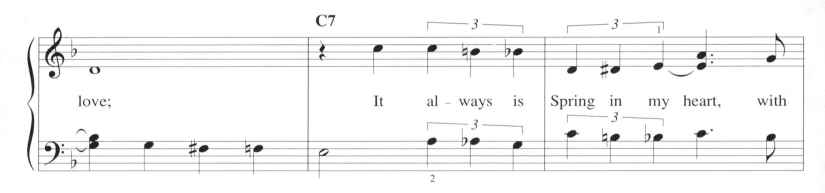

love; It al-ways is Spring in my heart, with

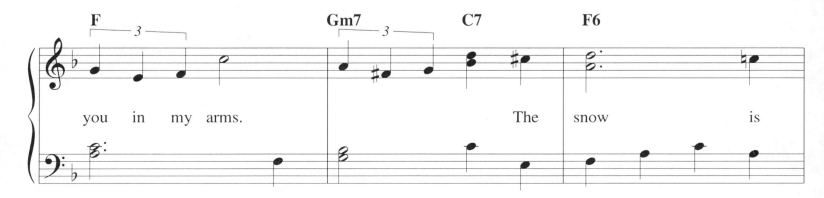

you in my arms. The snow is

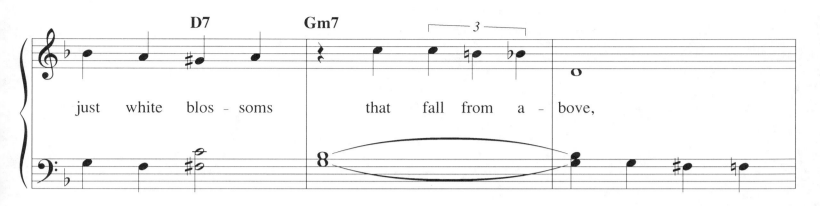

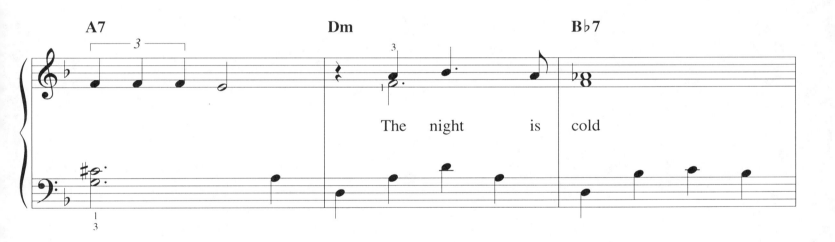

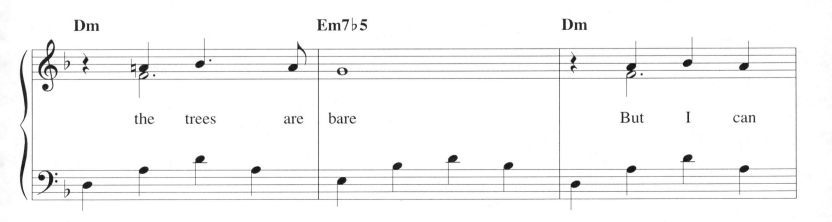

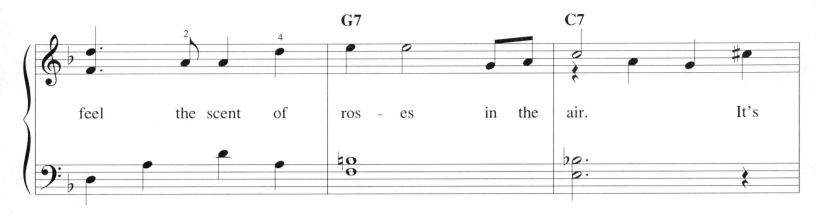

feel the scent of ros — es in the air. It's

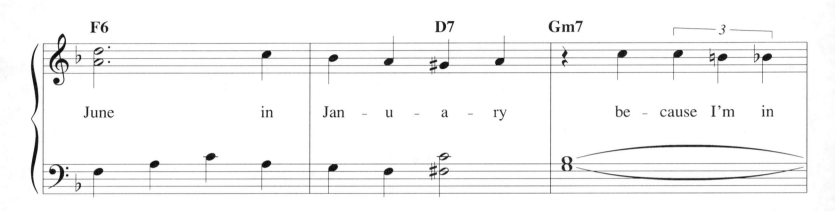

June in Jan - u - a - ry be - cause I'm in

love, But on - ly be - cause I'm in love with

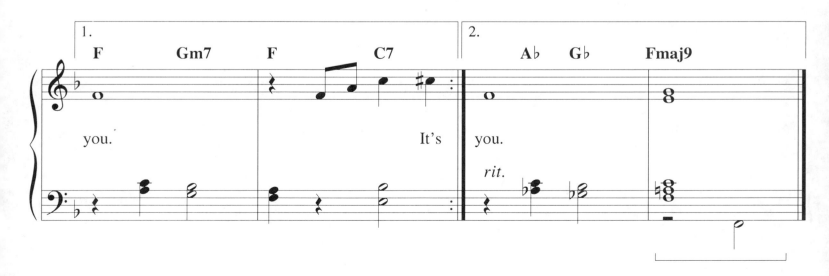

you. It's you. you.

JUST ONE MORE CHANCE

Words by SAM COSLOW
Music by ARTHUR JOHNSTON

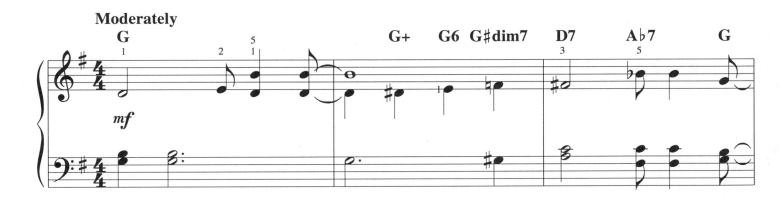

Just one more chance,

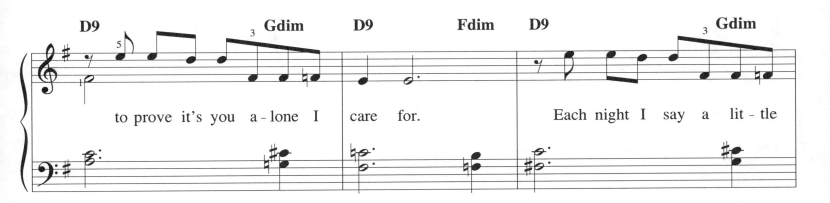

to prove it's you a-lone I care for. Each night I say a lit-tle

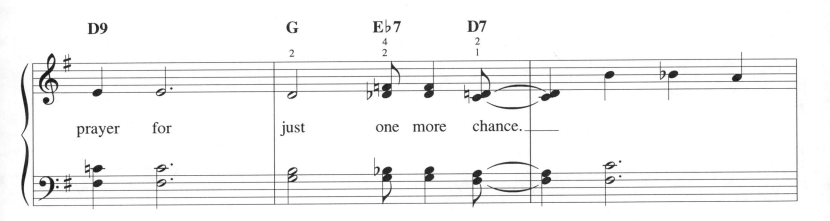

prayer for just one more chance.

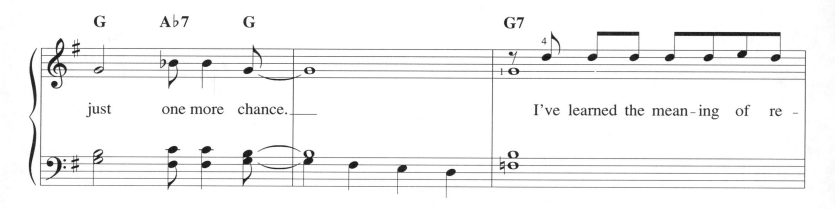

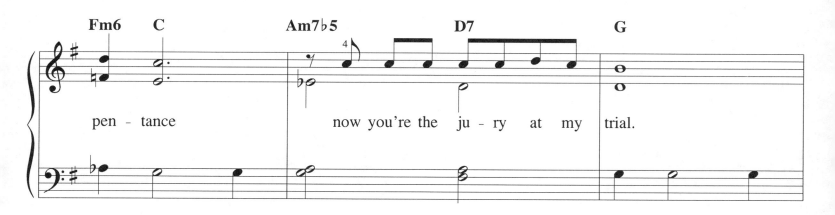

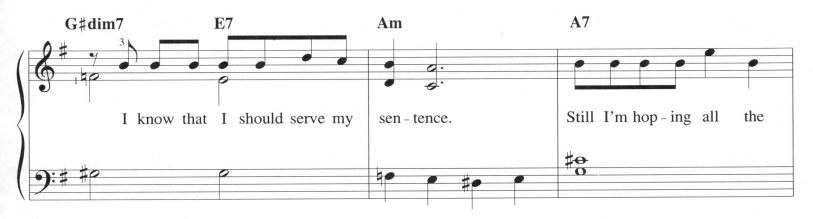

I know that I should serve my sen - tence. Still I'm hop - ing all the

while you'll give me just one more word.

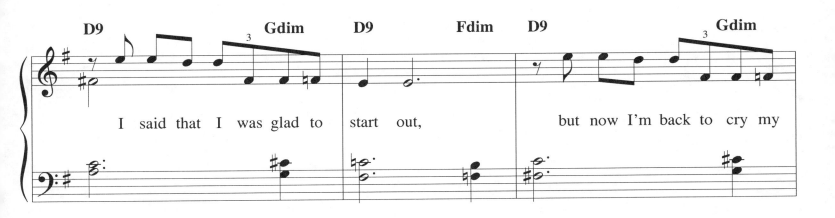

I said that I was glad to start out, but now I'm back to cry my

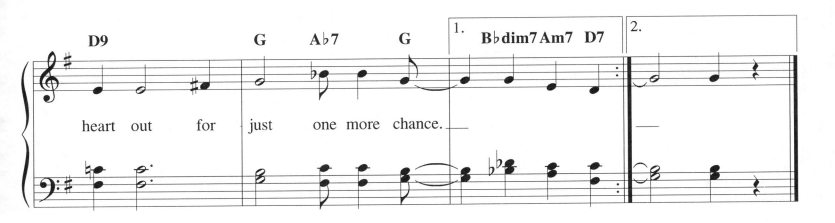

heart out for just one more chance.

LET'S FACE THE MUSIC AND DANCE

from the Motion Picture FOLLOW THE FLEET

Words and Music by
IRVING BERLIN

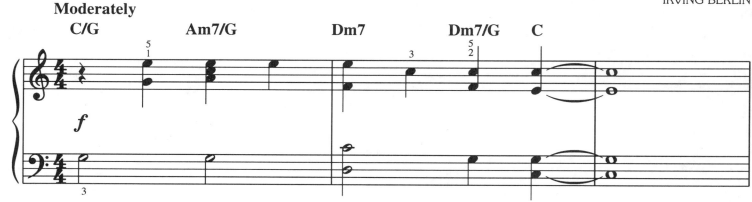

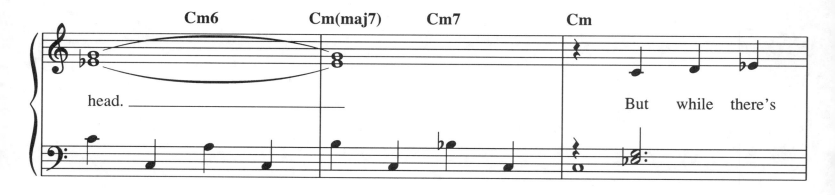

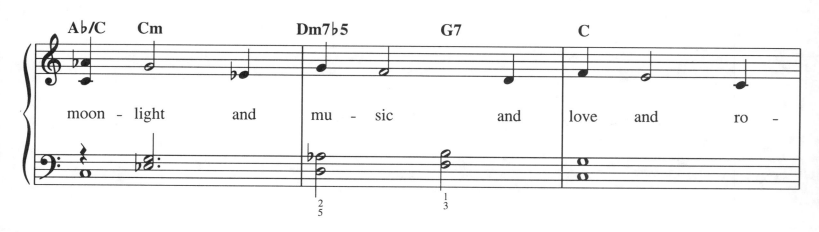

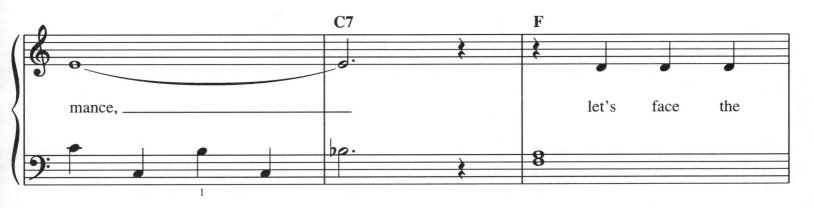

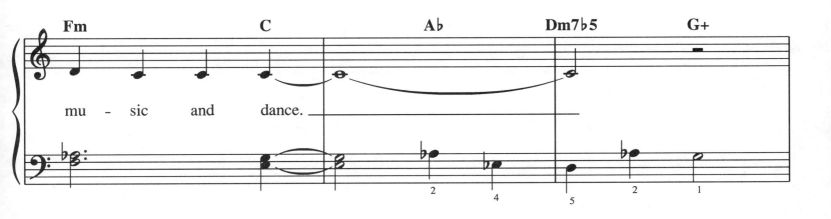

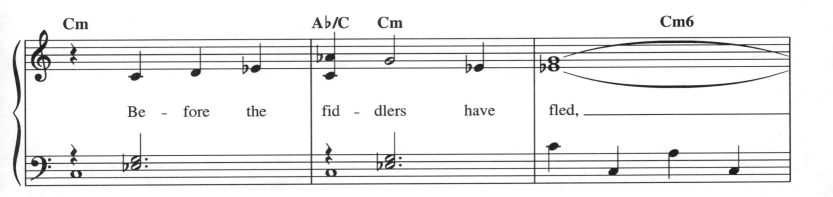

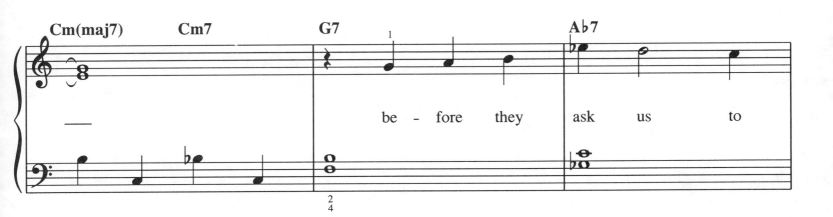

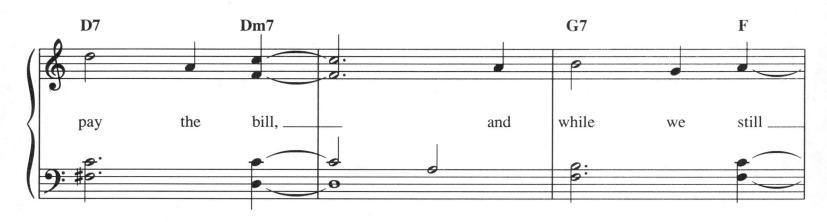

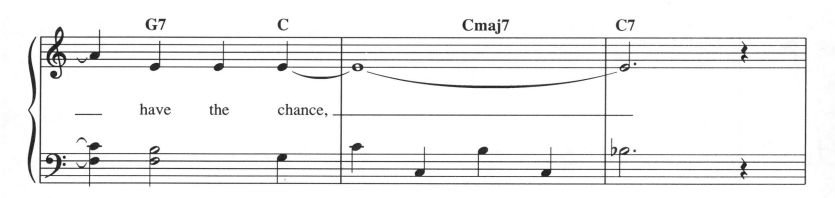

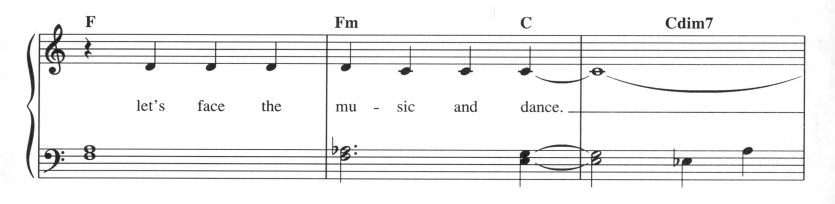

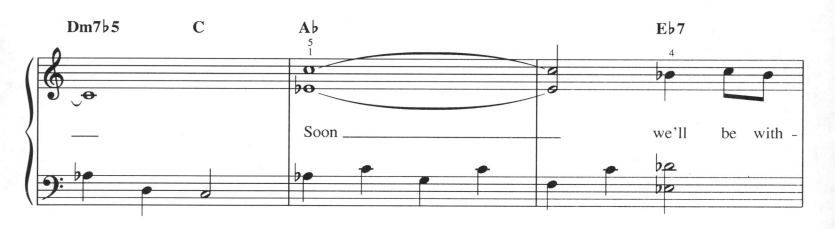

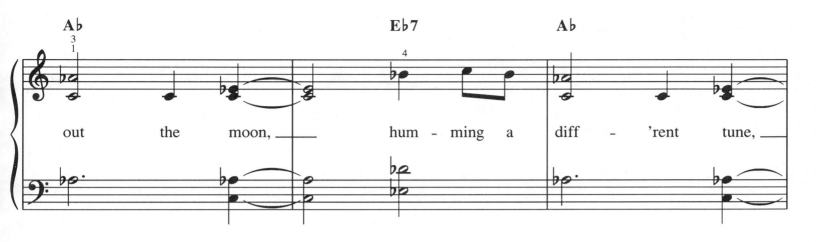

out the moon, _____ hum - ming a diff - 'rent tune, _____

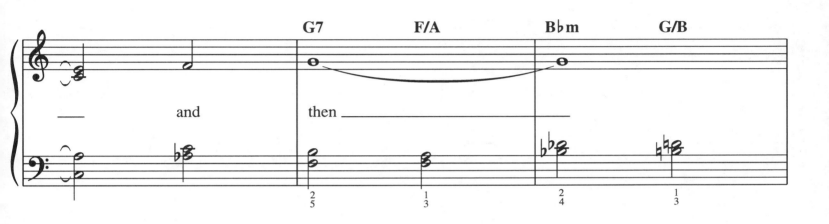

_____ and then _____

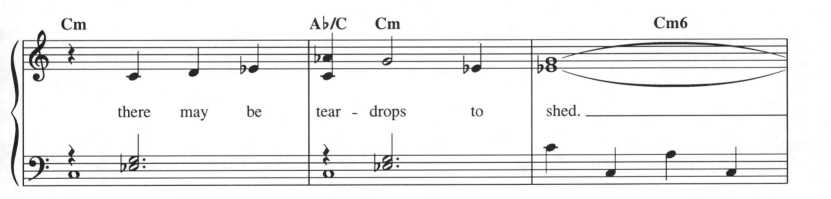

there may be tear - drops to shed. _____

_____ So while there's moon - light and

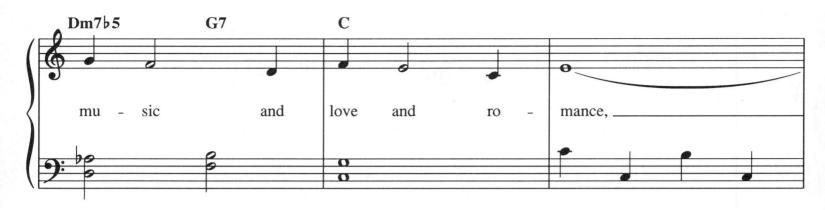

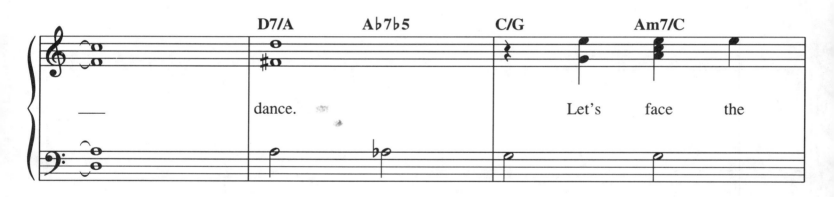

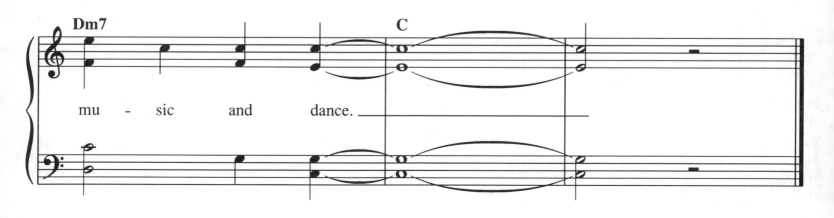

LOVE IS JUST AROUND THE CORNER

from the Paramount Picture HERE IS MY HEART

Words and Music by LEO ROBIN
and LEWIS E. GENSLER

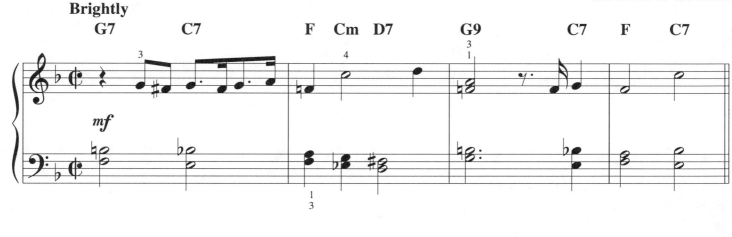

Love is just a-round the cor - ner, an - y co - zy lit - tle

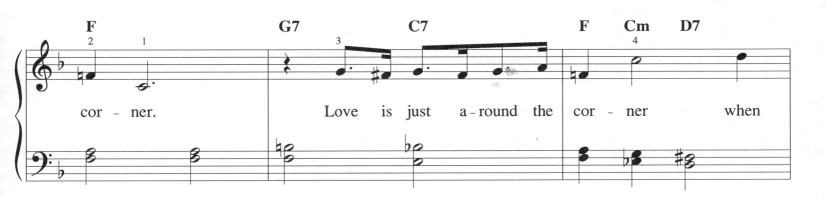

cor - ner. Love is just a-round the cor - ner when

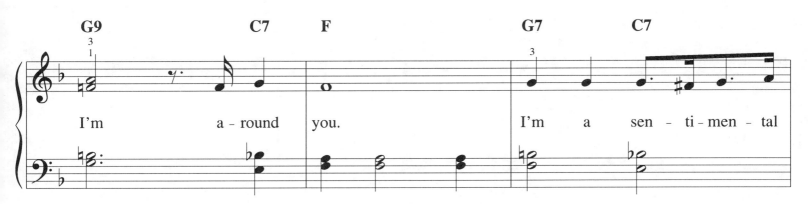

I'm a - round you. I'm a sen - ti - men - tal

mourn – er   and I could – n't be for – lorn – er,

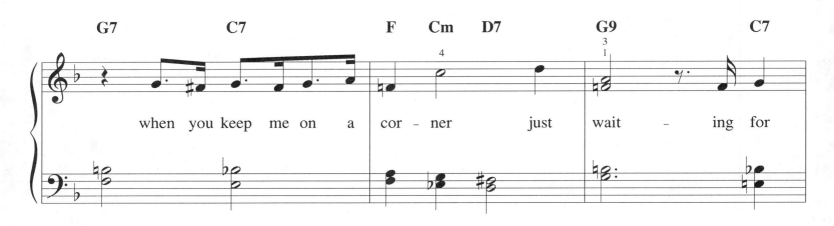

when you keep me on a cor – ner   just wait – ing for

you. _____   Ve – nus de Mi – lo was not – ed for her

charms.   But strict – ly be – tween us you're cut – er than Ve – nus and

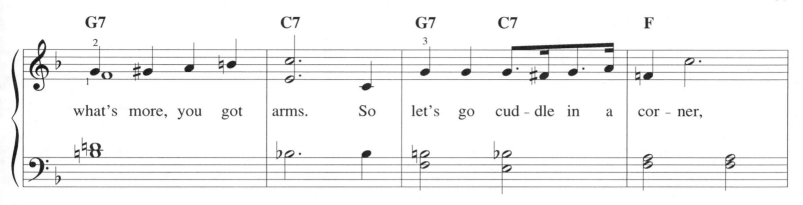

what's more, you got arms. So let's go cud - dle in a cor - ner,

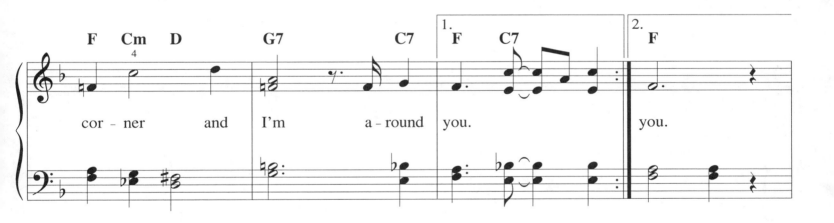

an - y co - zy lit - tle cor - ner. Love is just a-round the

cor - ner and I'm a - round you. you.

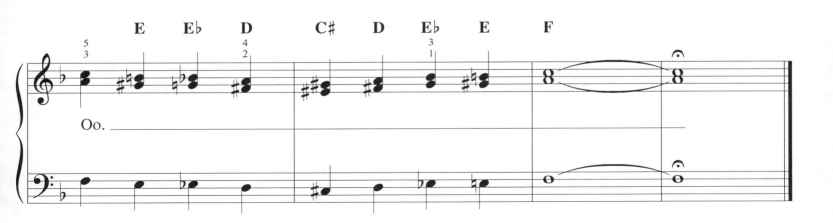

Oo. _____

LOVE ME OR LEAVE ME

from LOVE ME OR LEAVE ME

Lyrics by GUS KAHN
Music by WALTER DONALDSON

Gm　　　　　　　　　　　　**A7**　　**D7**　　　　**B♭**

night-time　is　my　time　for　just　rem - i - nis-cing,　re - gret-ting,　in-stead　of　for -

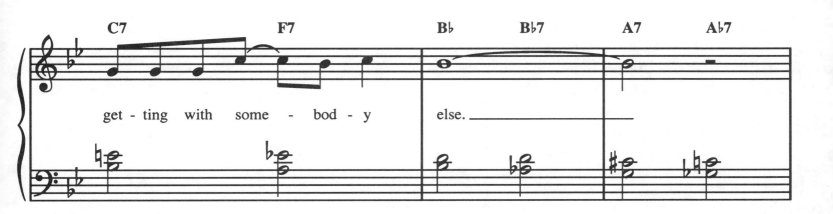

C7　　　　　　　**F7**　　　　　　**B♭**　　**B♭7**　　　**A7**　　**A♭7**

get - ting　with　some - bod - y　else. ____

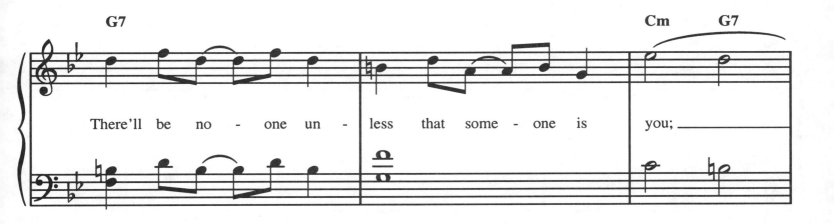

G7　　　　　　　　　　　　　　　　　　　　　　**Cm**　　**G7**

There'll　be　no - one　un - less　that　some - one　is　you; ____

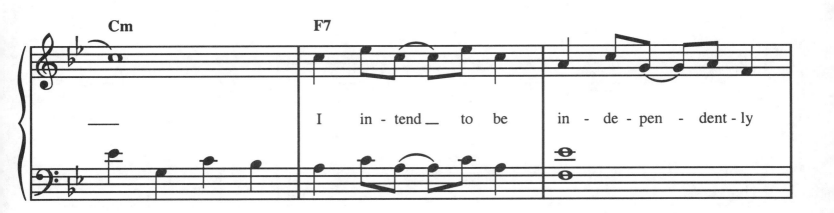

Cm　　　　　　　　**F7**

____　I　in - tend ___ to　be　in - de - pen - dent - ly

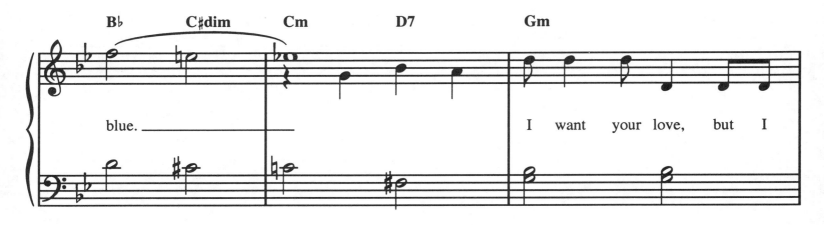

blue. _____

I want your love, but I

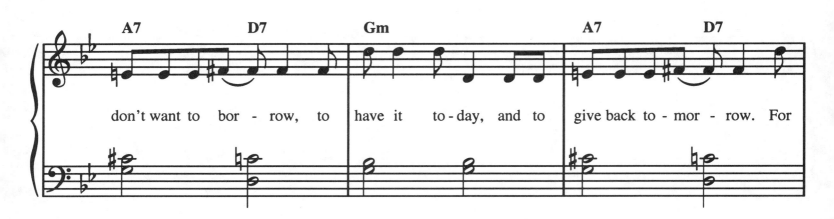

don't want to bor - row, to have it to - day, and to give back to - mor - row. For

my love is your love, there's no love for no - bod - y else!

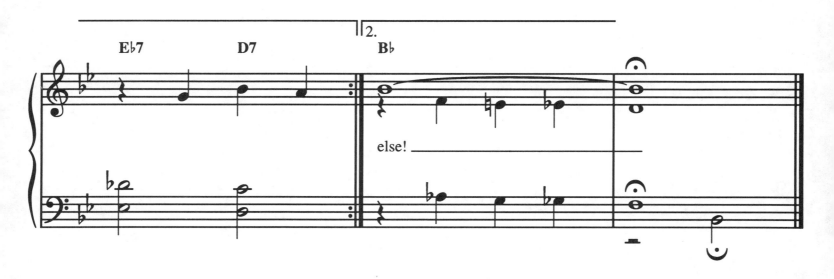

else! _____

MAKIN' WHOOPEE!
from WHOOPEE!

Lyrics by GUS KAHN
Music by WALTER DONALDSON

ner - vous, ___ he an-swers twice. _____ It's real - ly kill - ing ___ that he's so
phone her, ___ he does-n't write. _____ He says he's "bus - y," ___ but she says

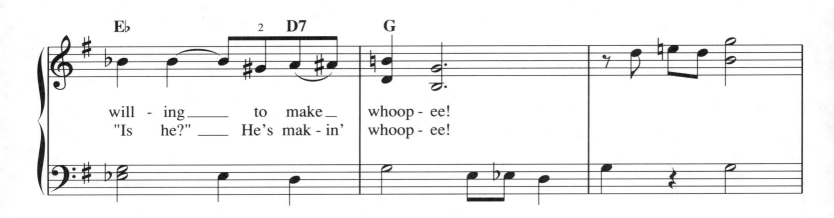

will - ing ___ to make ___ whoop - ee!
"Is he?" ___ He's mak - in' whoop - ee!

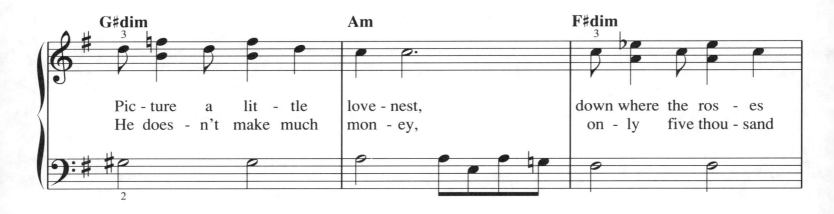

Pic - ture a lit - tle love - nest, down where the ros - es
He does - n't make much mon - ey, on - ly five thou - sand

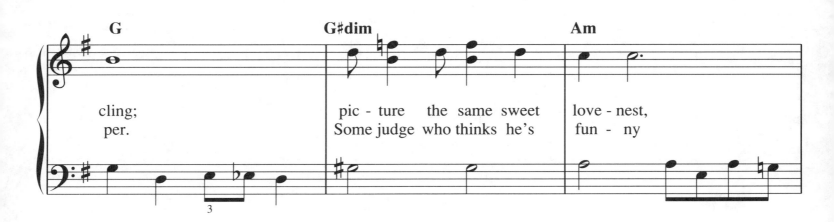

cling; pic - ture the same sweet love - nest,
per. Some judge who thinks he's fun - ny

MAKE BELIEVE
from SHOW BOAT

Lyrics by OSCAR HAMMERSTEIN II
Music by JEROME KERN

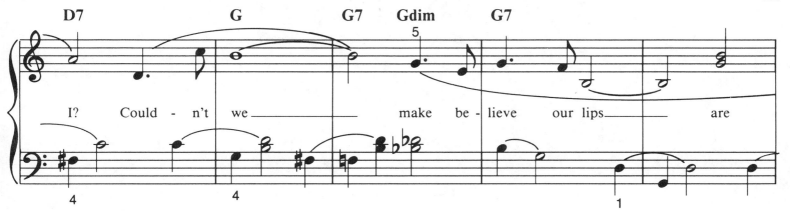

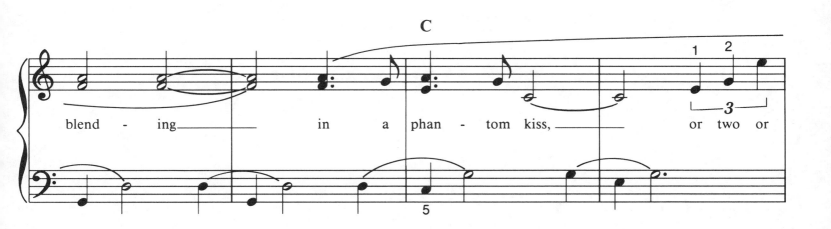

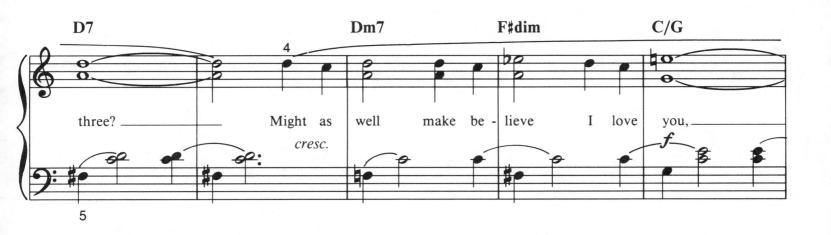

MEMORIES OF YOU
from THE BENNY GOODMAN STORY

Lyric by ANDY RAZAF
Music by EUBIE BLAKE

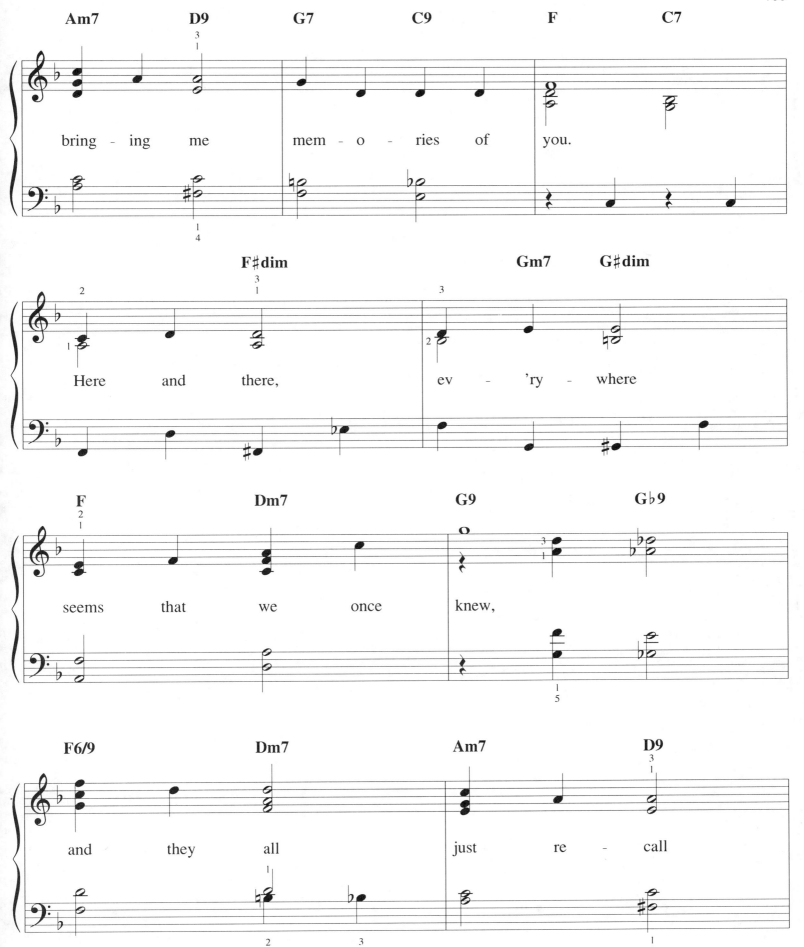

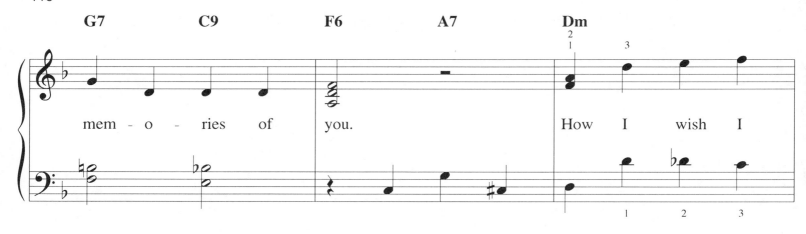

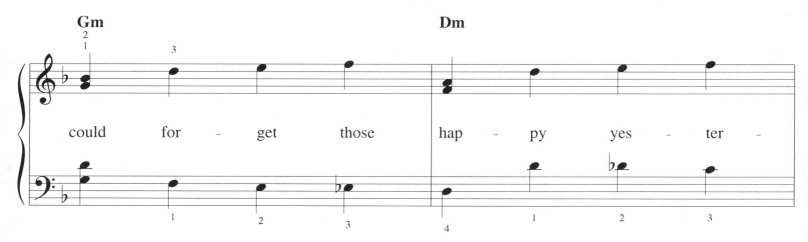

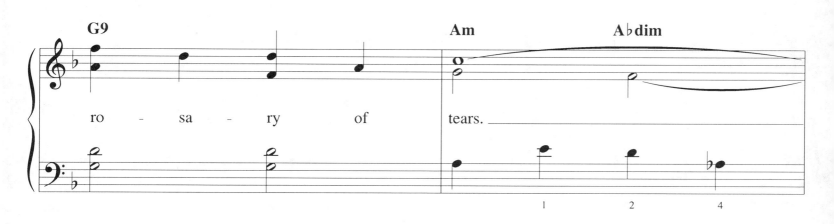

MOONLIGHT AND ROSES
(Bring Mem'ries of You)

Words and Music by BEN BLACK,
EDWIN H. LEMARE and NEIL MORET

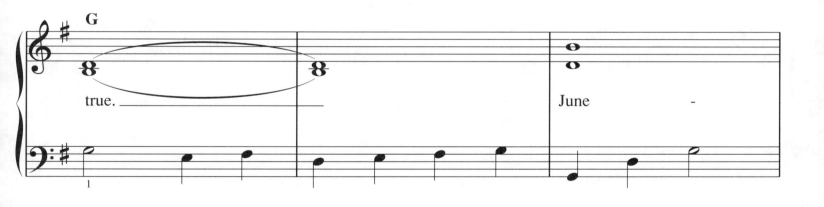

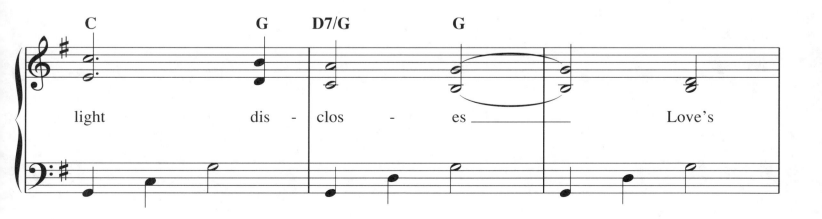

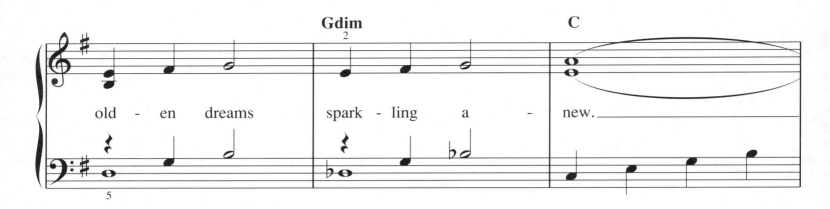

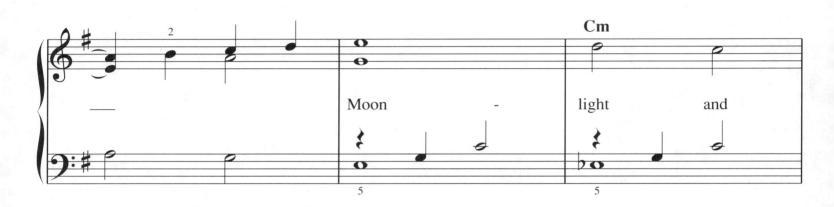

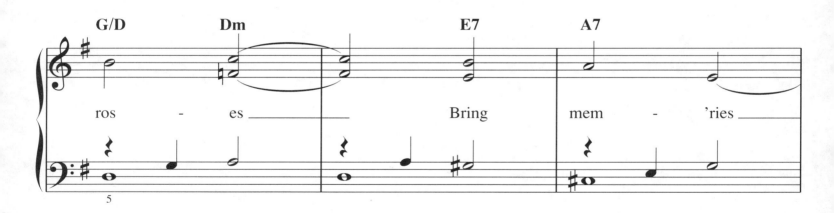

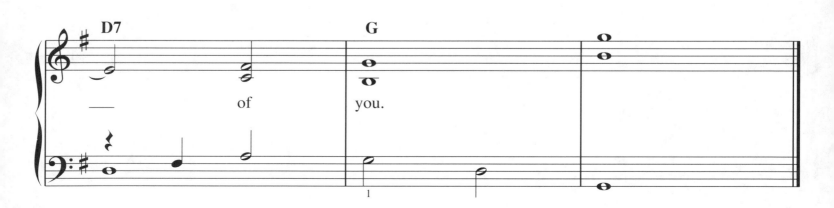

MORE THAN YOU KNOW

Words by WILLIAM ROSE and EDWARD ELISCU
Music by VINCENT YOUMANS

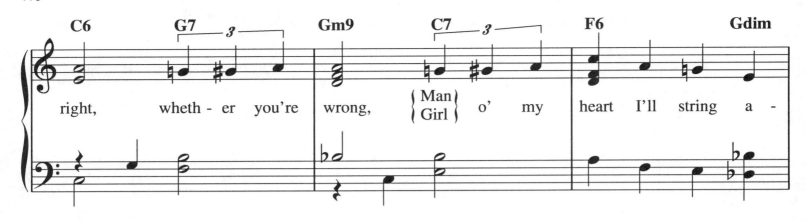

right,   wheth - er you're wrong,   {Man Girl} o' my   heart I'll string a -

long.   You need me   so   more than you'll ev - er   know.

Lov - ing you the   way that I   do there's   noth - ing I can do a -

bout it. _____   Lov - ing may be   all   you can give but

MY BLUE HEAVEN

Lyric by GEORGE WHITING
Music by WALTER DONALDSON

a lit - tle white light will lead me to

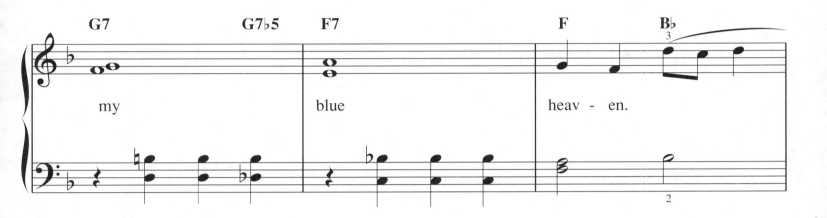

my blue heav - en.

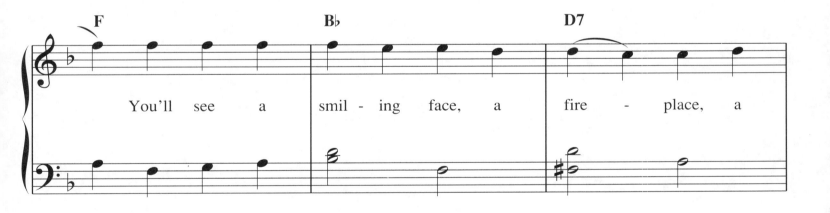

You'll see a smil - ing face, a fire - place, a

co - zy room, a lit - tle nest that's

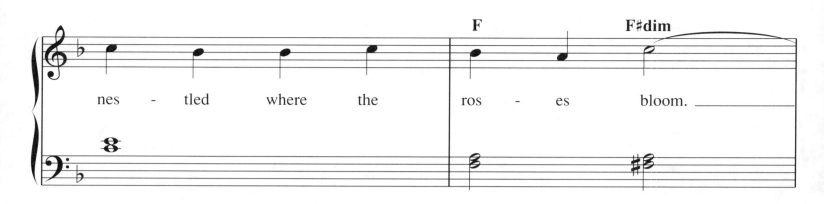

nes - tled   where   the   ros - es   bloom. _____

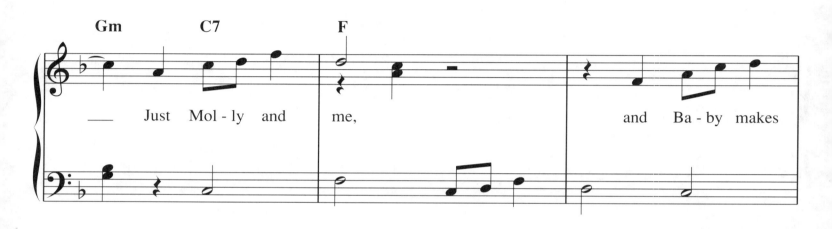

_____ Just Mol - ly and   me,   and Ba - by makes

three.   We're hap - py in   my

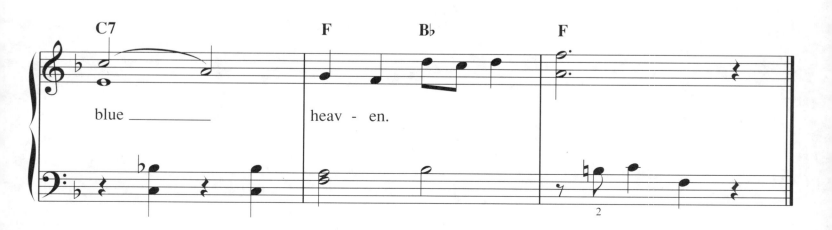

blue _____   heav - en.

MY FUNNY VALENTINE

from BABES IN ARMS

Words and LORENZ HART
Music by RICHARD RODGERS

Slowly

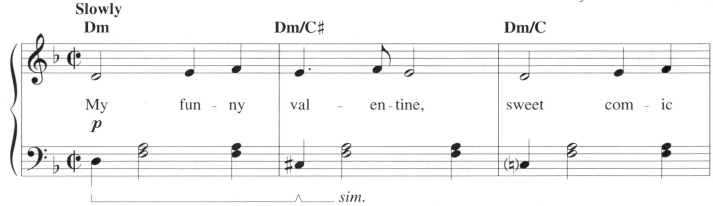

My fun-ny val - en-tine, sweet com - ic

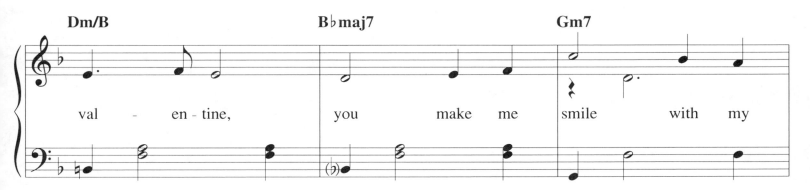

val - en-tine, you make me smile with my

heart. Your looks are

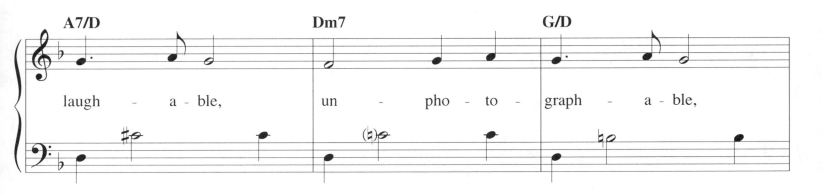

laugh - a - ble, un - pho - to - graph - a - ble,

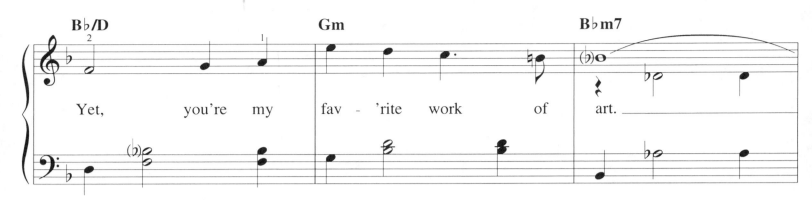

Yet, you're my fav - 'rite work of art. _____

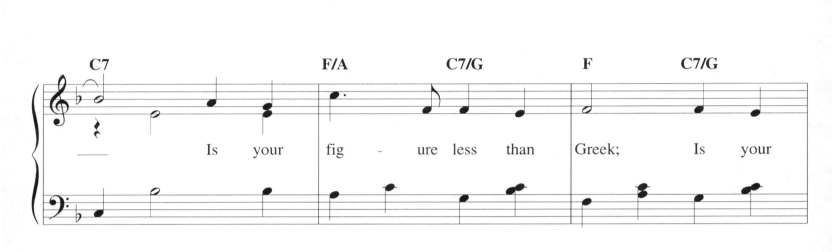

_____ Is your fig - ure less than Greek; Is your

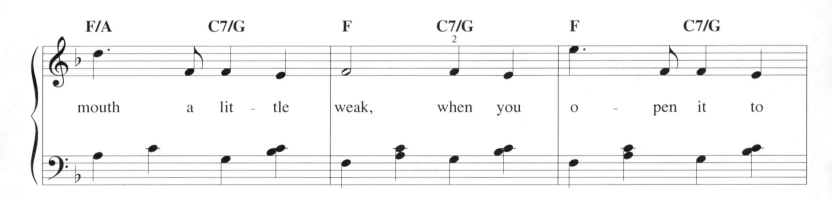

mouth a lit - tle weak, when you o - pen it to

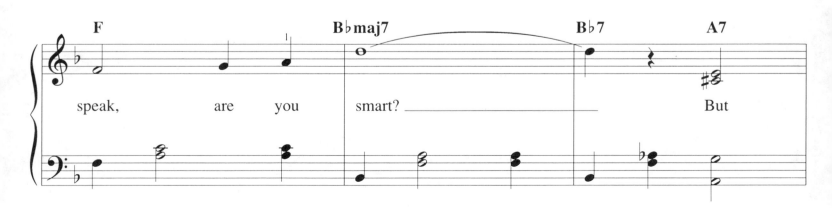

speak, are you smart? _____ But

don't change a hair for me, not if you

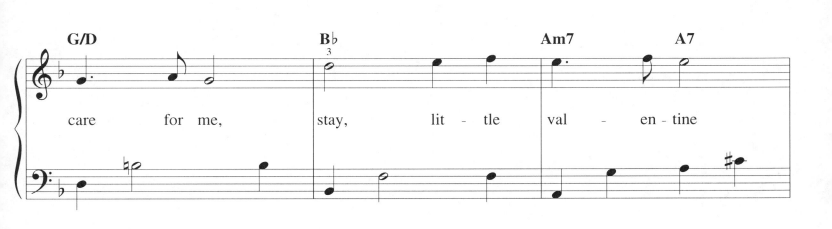

care for me, stay, lit - tle val - en - tine

stay! _____ Each day is

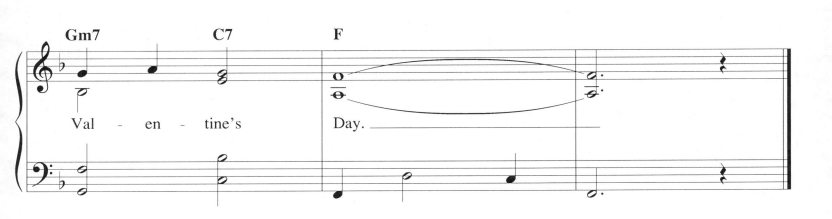

Val - en - tine's Day. _____

MY HEART STOOD STILL

from A CONNECTICUT YANKEE

Words by LORENZ HART
Music by RICHARD RODGERS

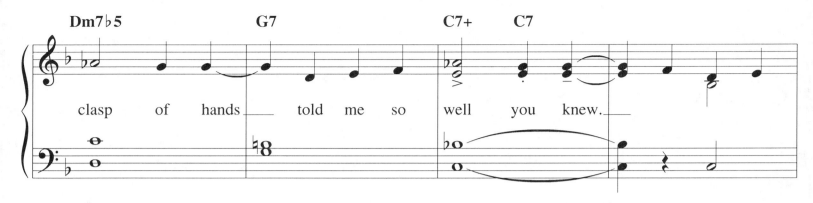

126

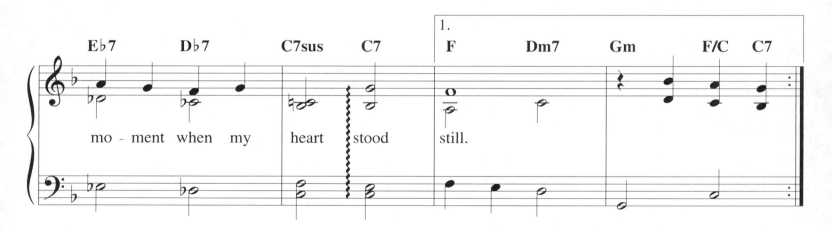

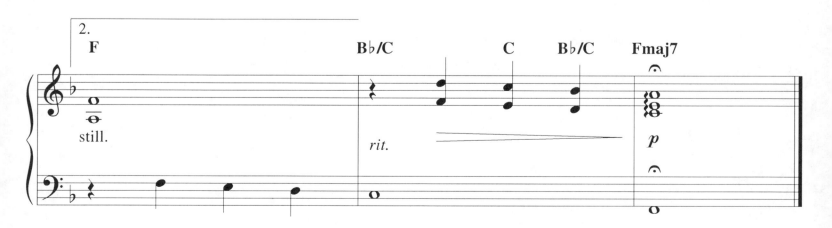

MY ROMANCE
from JUMBO

Words by LORENZ HART
Music by RICHARD RODGERS

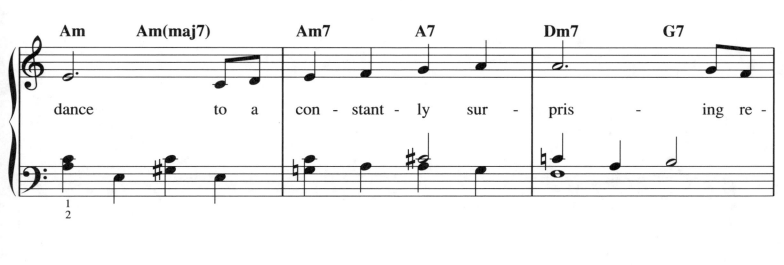

dance to a con - stant - ly sur - pris - ing re -

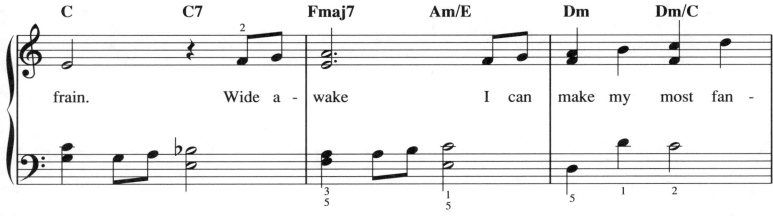

frain. Wide a - wake I can make my most fan -

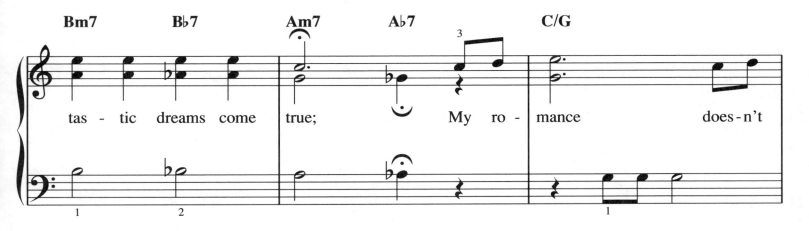

tas - tic dreams come true; My ro - mance does-n't

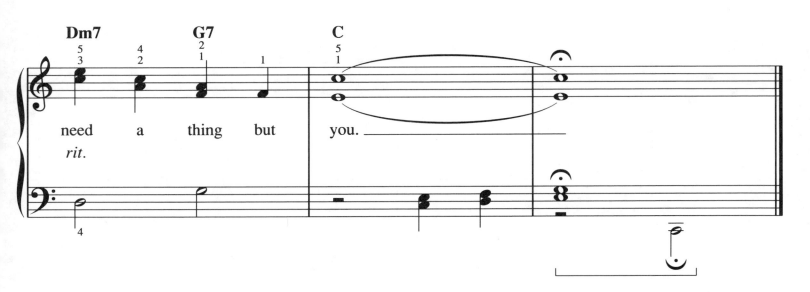

need a thing but you. _____

rit.

MY IDEAL

from the Paramount Picture PLAYBOY OF PARIS

Words by LEO ROBIN
Music by RICHARD A. WHITING
and NEWELL CHASE

RED SAILS IN THE SUNSET

Words by JIMMY KENNEDY
Music by HUGH WILLIAMS (WILL GROSZ)

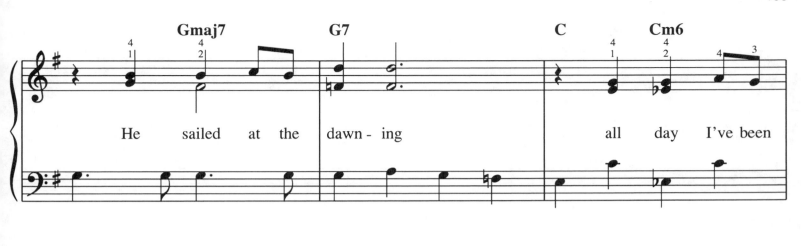

He sailed at the dawn - ing   all day I've been

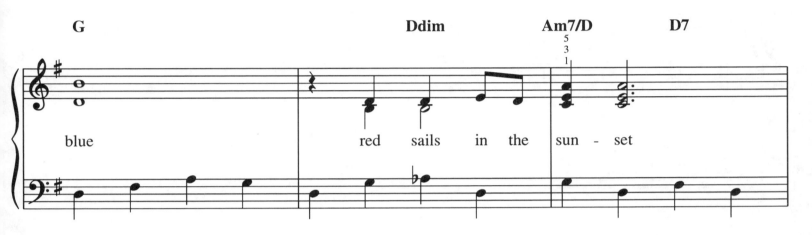

blue   red sails in the sun - set

I'm trust - ing in you.   Swift   wings you must

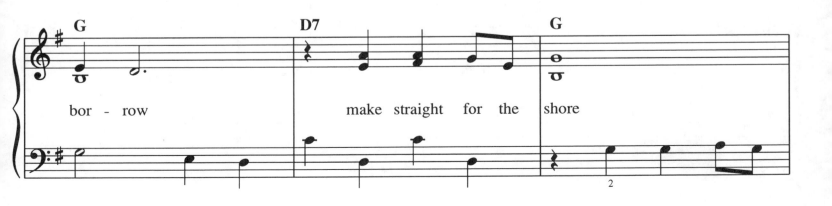

bor - row   make straight for the shore

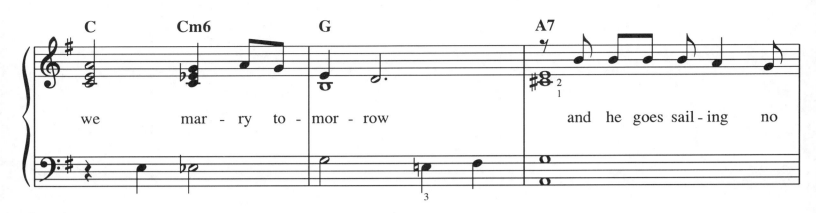

we mar - ry to - mor - row and he goes sail - ing no

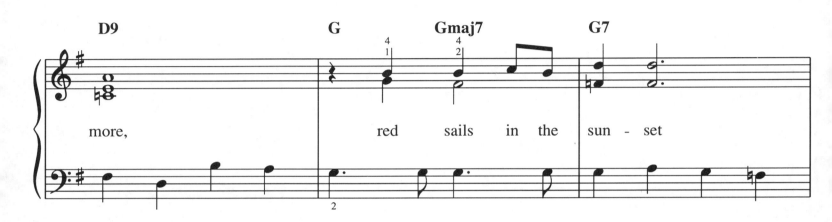

more, red sails in the sun - set

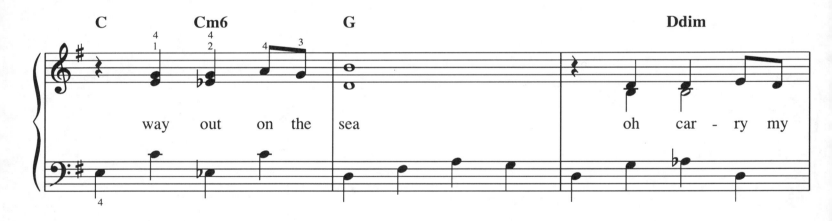

way out on the sea oh car - ry my

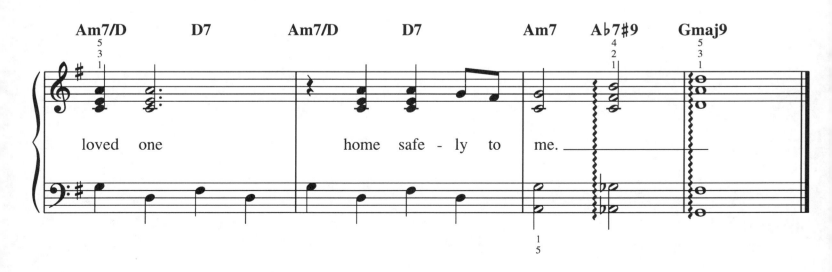

loved one home safe - ly to me.

SOFT LIGHTS AND SWEET MUSIC

from the Stage Production FACE THE MUSIC

Words and Music by
IRVING BERLIN

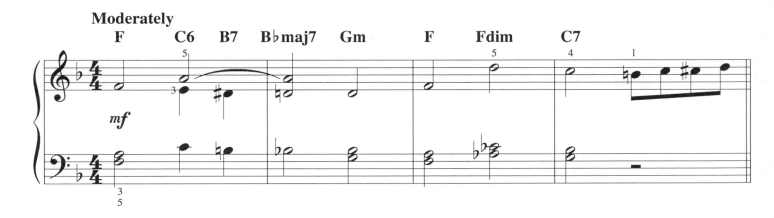

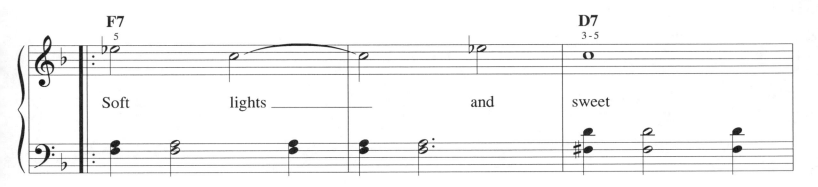

Soft   lights _____ and   sweet

mu - sic   and   you   in _____ my

arms. _____ Soft   lights   and

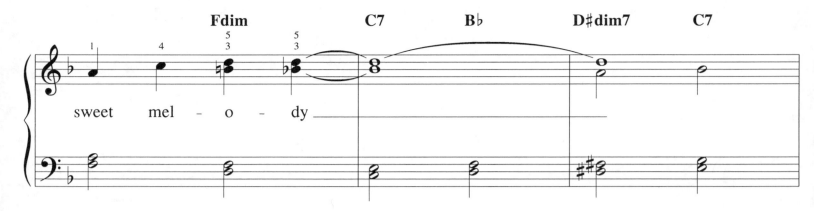

sweet mel – o – dy

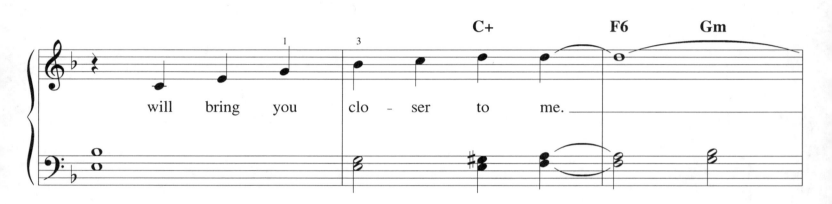

will bring you clo – ser to me.

Cho – pin and

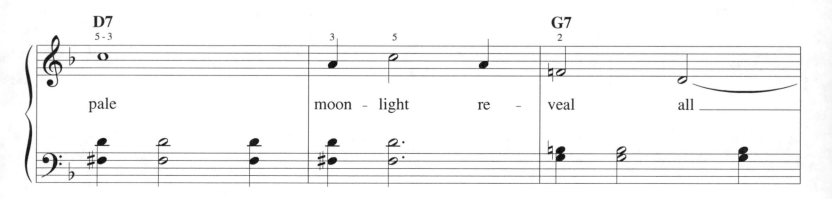

pale moon – light re – veal all

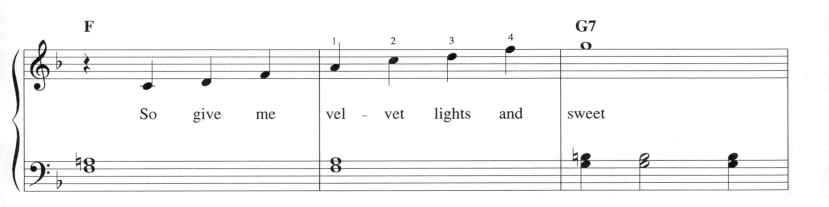

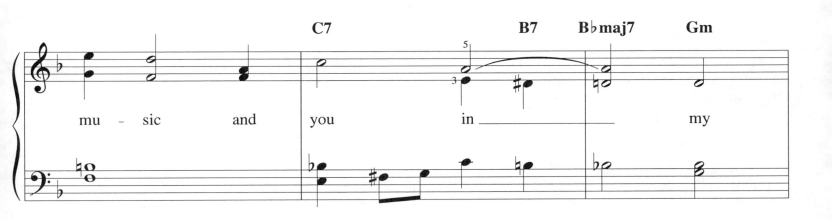

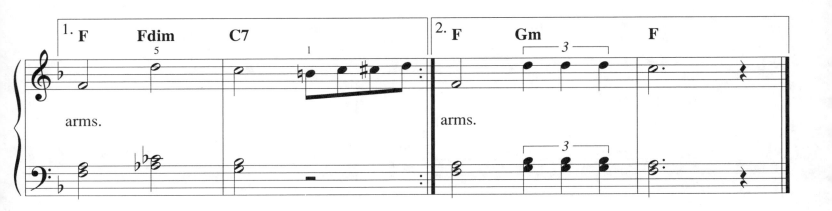

SEPTEMBER SONG
from the Musical Play KNICKERBOCKER HOLIDAY

Words by MAXWELL ANDERSON
Music by KURT WEILL

Moderately Slow

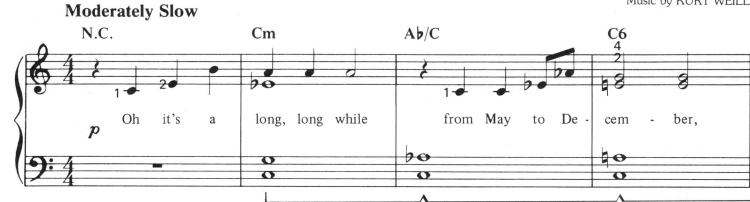

Oh it's a long, long while from May to De- cem- ber,

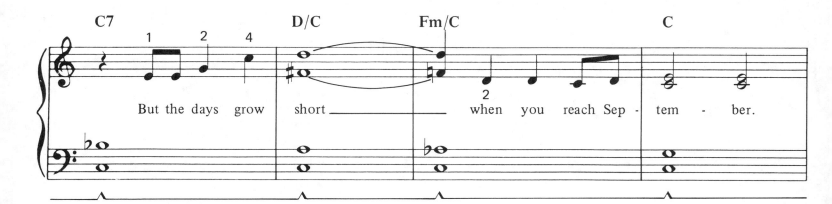

But the days grow short ___ when you reach Sep- tem- ber.

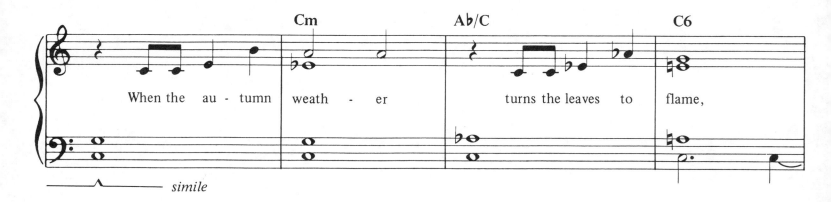

When the au- tumn weath- er turns the leaves to flame,

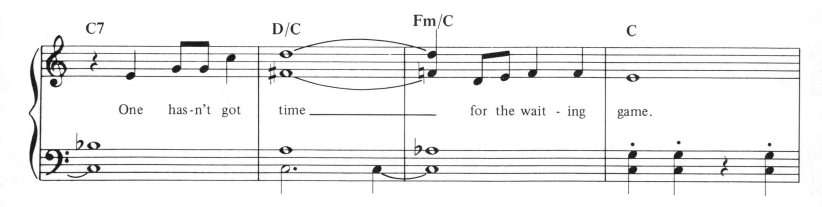

One has-n't got time ___ for the wait- ing game.

Oh, the days dwin-dle down _____ to a pre - cious few, _____

_____ Sep - tem - ber, _____ No - vem - ber!

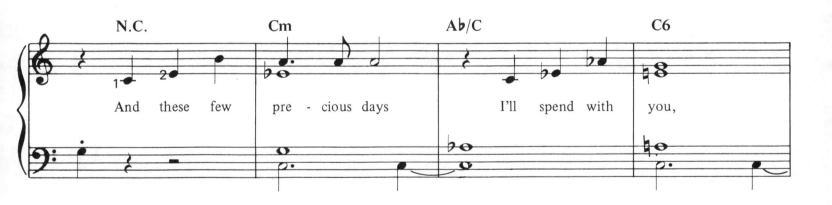

And these few pre - cious days   I'll spend with   you,

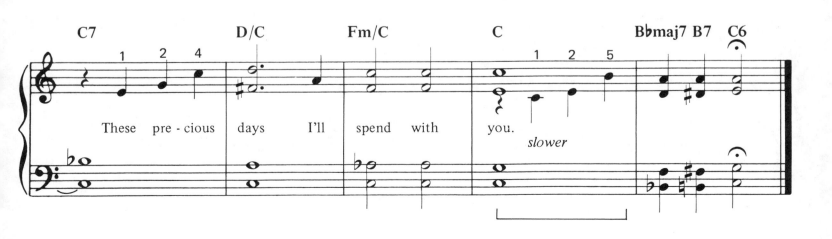

These pre - cious days   I'll   spend with   you.

slower

STAR DUST

Words by MITCHELL PARISH
Music by HOAGY CARMICHAEL

Slowly

And now the pur-ple dusk of twi-light time

Steals a-cross the mead-ows of my heart; High up in the sky the

lit-tle stars climb, al-ways re-mind-ing me that we're a-part.

You wan-dered down the lane and far a-way, Leav-ing me a song that will not

die;   Love is now the star dust   of   yes-ter-day,

The mu-sic of the years gone   by._____ Some-times I   won - der why I

spend the lone - ly   night   dream-ing of a song.   The

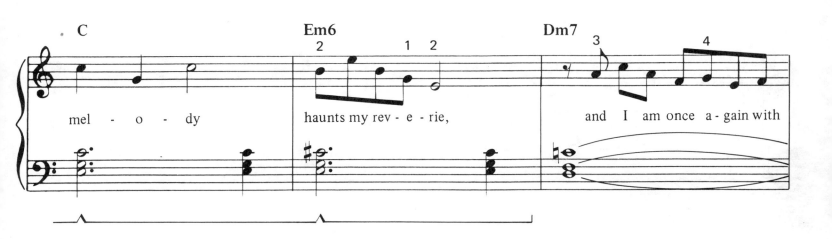

mel - o - dy   haunts my rev-e-rie,   and I am once a-gain with

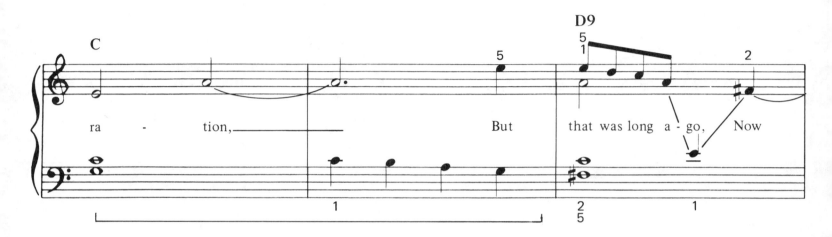

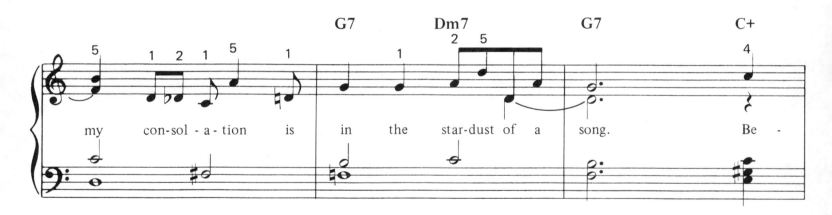

night - in - gale   tells his fair - y tale   of par - a - dise where ros-es

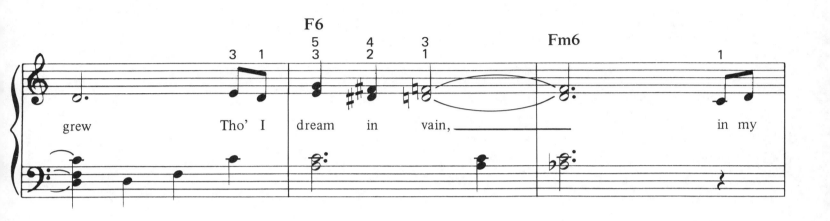

grew   Tho' I dream in vain, _____   in my

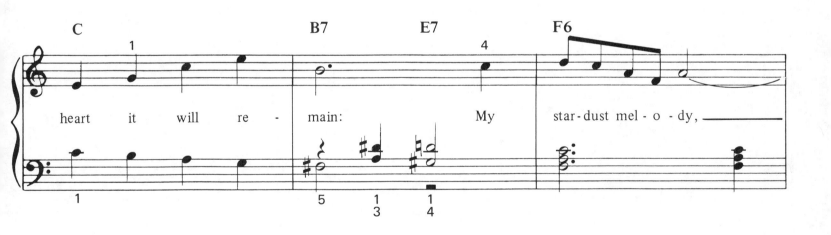

heart it will re - main: My   star-dust mel - o - dy, _____

_____ the mem - o - ry   of love's re - frain.

rall.

THERE'S A SMALL HOTEL

from ON YOUR TOES

Words by LORENZ HART
Music by RICHARD RODGERS

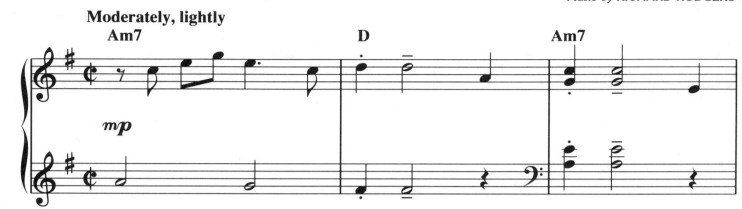

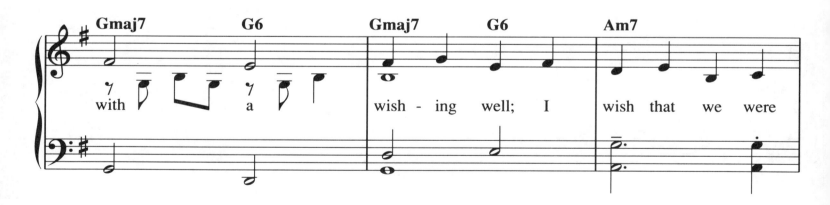

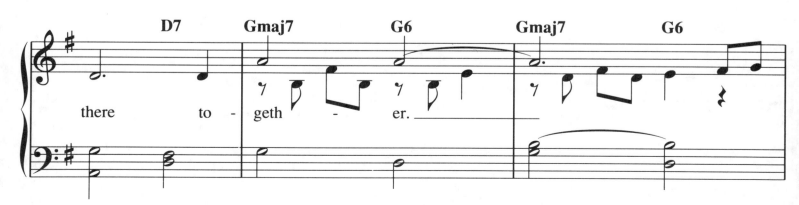

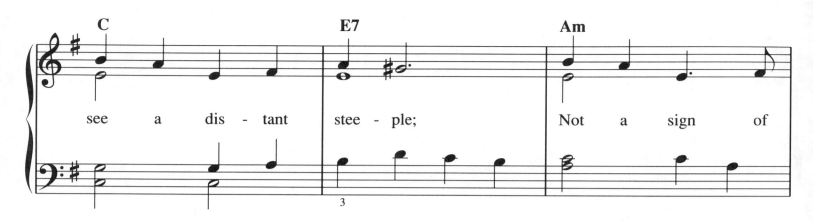

see a dis - tant stee - ple; Not a sign of

peo - ple, Who wants peo - ple?

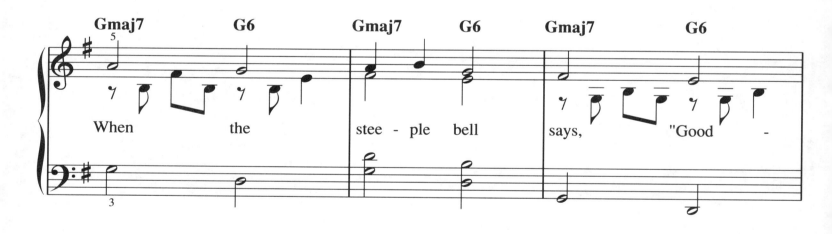

When the stee - ple bell says, "Good -

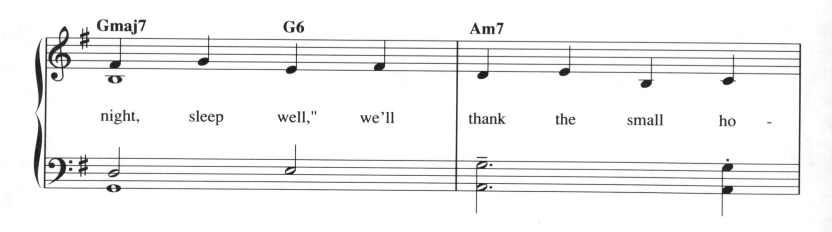

night, sleep well," we'll thank the small ho -

THOU SWELL

from A CONNECTICUT YANKEE
from WORDS AND MUSIC

Words by LORENZ HART
Music by RICHARD RODGERS

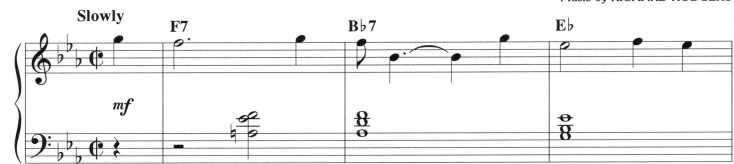

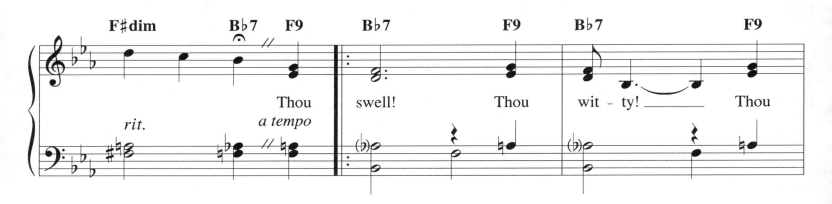

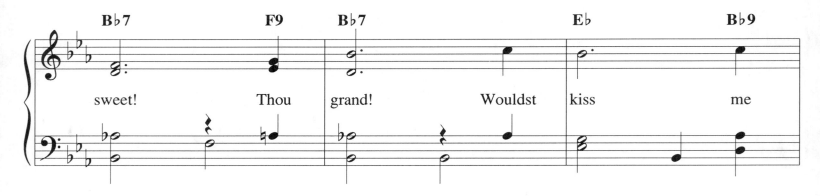

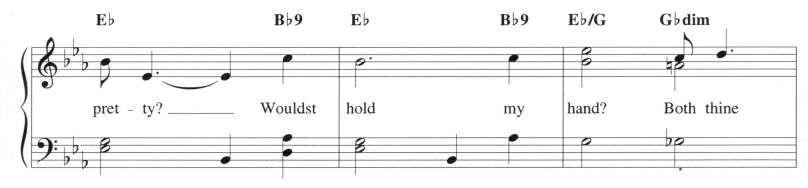

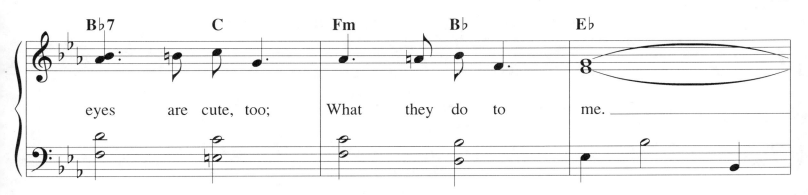

eyes   are cute, too;   What   they do to   me.

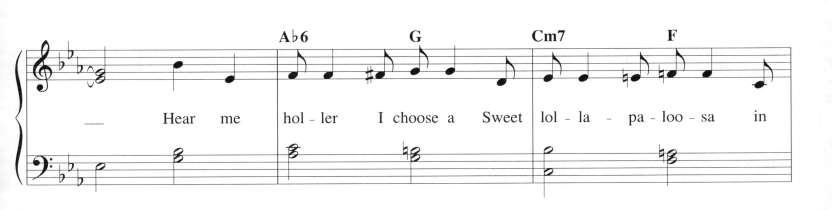

___ Hear me hol - ler I choose a Sweet lol - la - pa - loo - sa in

thee.   I'd   feel   so

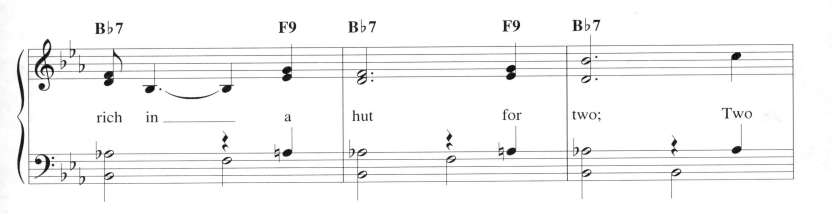

rich in _____ a   hut   for   two;   Two

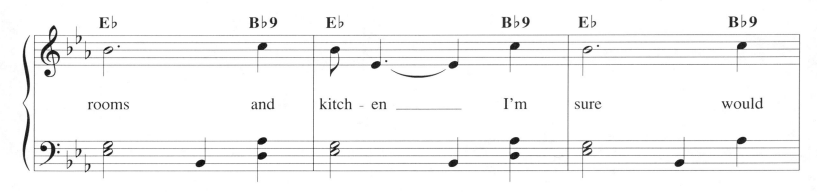

rooms   and   kitch - en _____ I'm   sure   would

do;   Give me   just   a   plot of,   Not   a   lot of

land,   And   Thou   swell!   Thou   wit - ty! _____ Thou

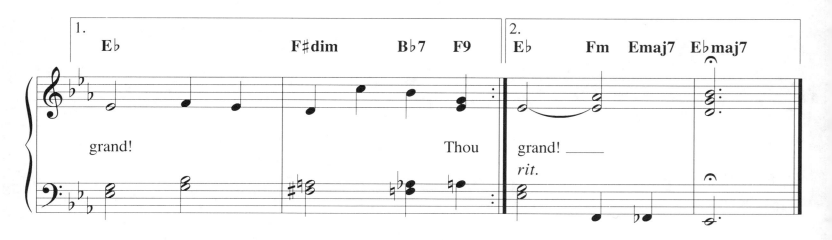

grand!   Thou   grand! _____

THE VERY THOUGHT OF YOU

Words and Music by
RAY NOBLE

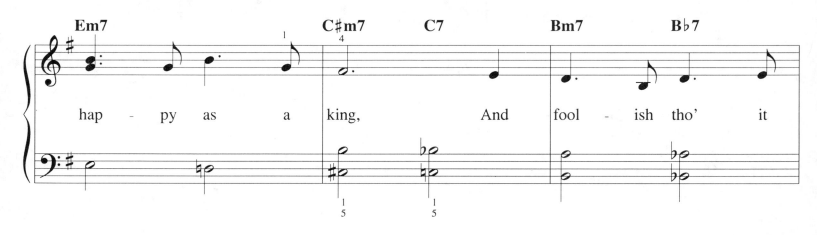

hap - py as a king, And fool - ish tho' it

may seem, To me _____ that's ev - 'ry - thing. _____ The mere i -
a tempo

dea of you, The long-ing here for you,

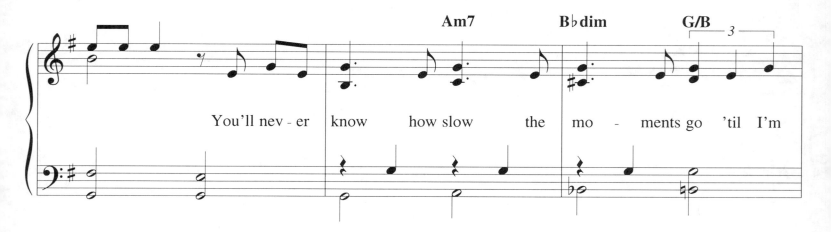

You'll nev - er know how slow the mo - ments go 'til I'm

The Way You Look Tonight
from SWING TIME

Words by DOROTHY FIELDS
Music by JEROME KERN

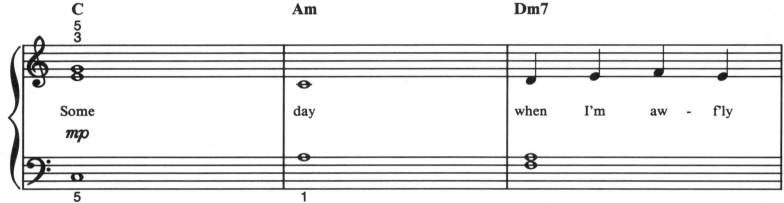

Some day when I'm aw-f'ly low,

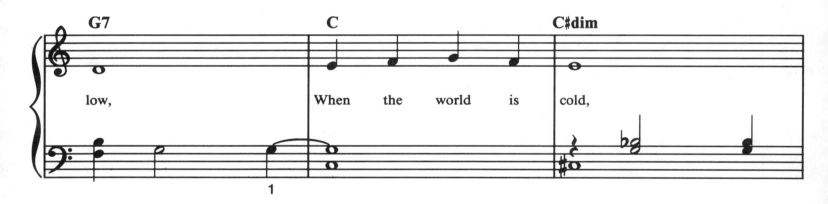

When the world is cold,

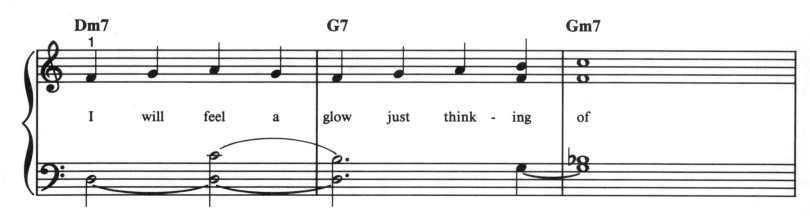

I will feel a glow just think-ing of

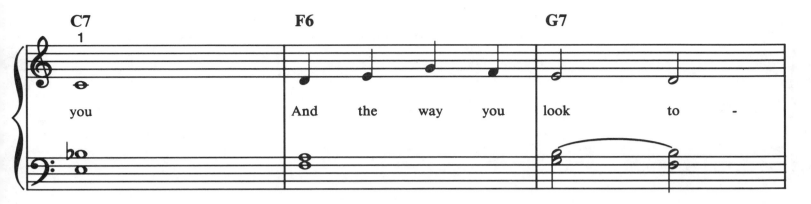

you And the way you look to -

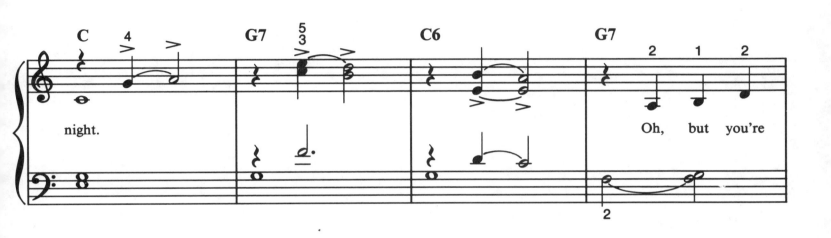

night. Oh, but you're

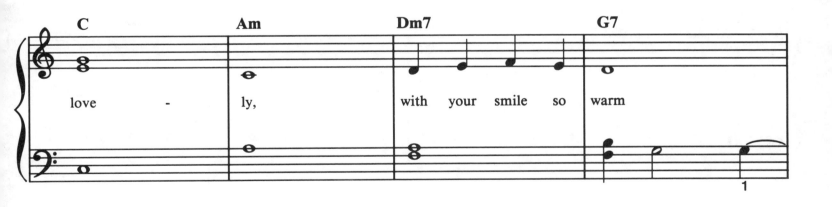

love - ly, with your smile so warm

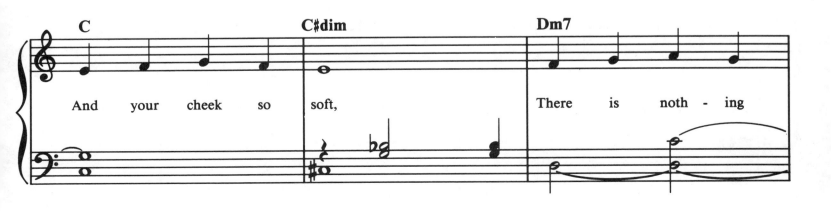

And your cheek so soft, There is noth - ing

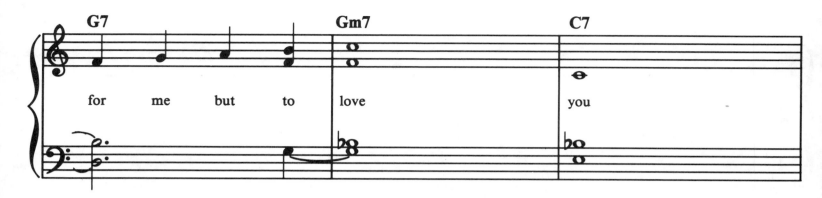

for me but to love you

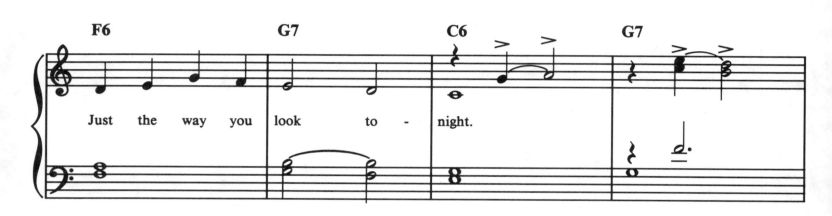

Just the way you look to - night.

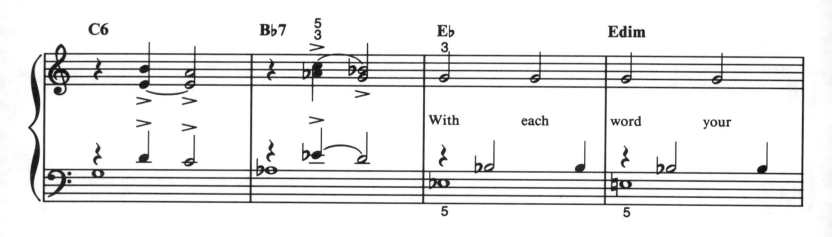

With each word your

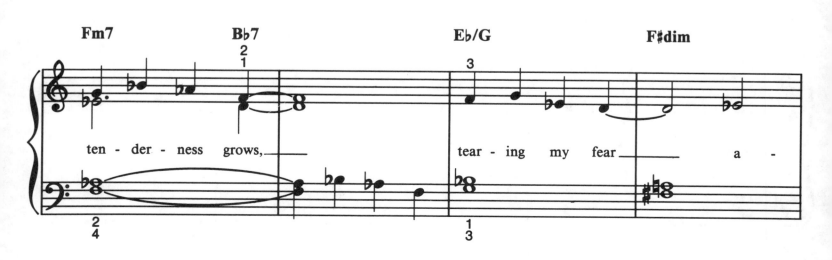

ten - der - ness grows, tear - ing my fear a -

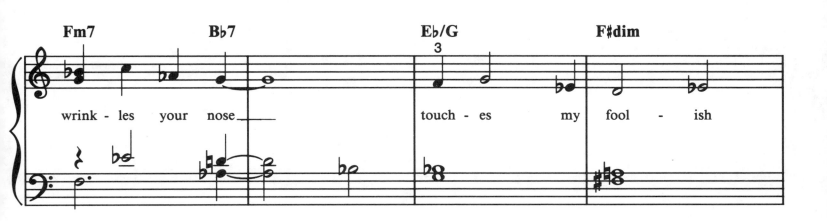

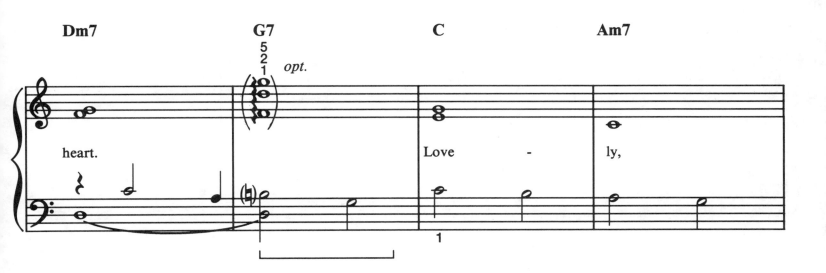

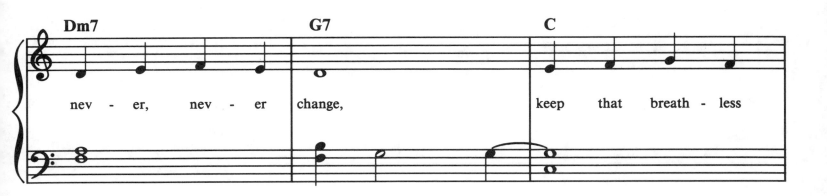

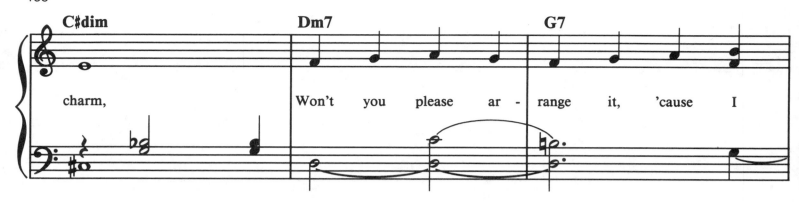

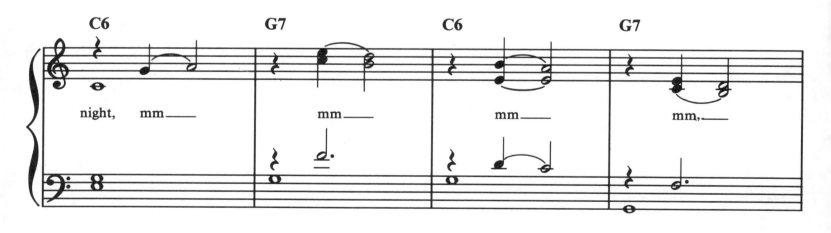

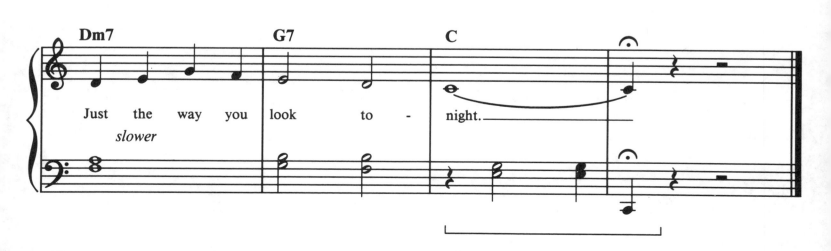

WHAT'LL I DO?
from MUSIC BOX REVUE OF 1924

Words and Music by
IRVING BERLIN

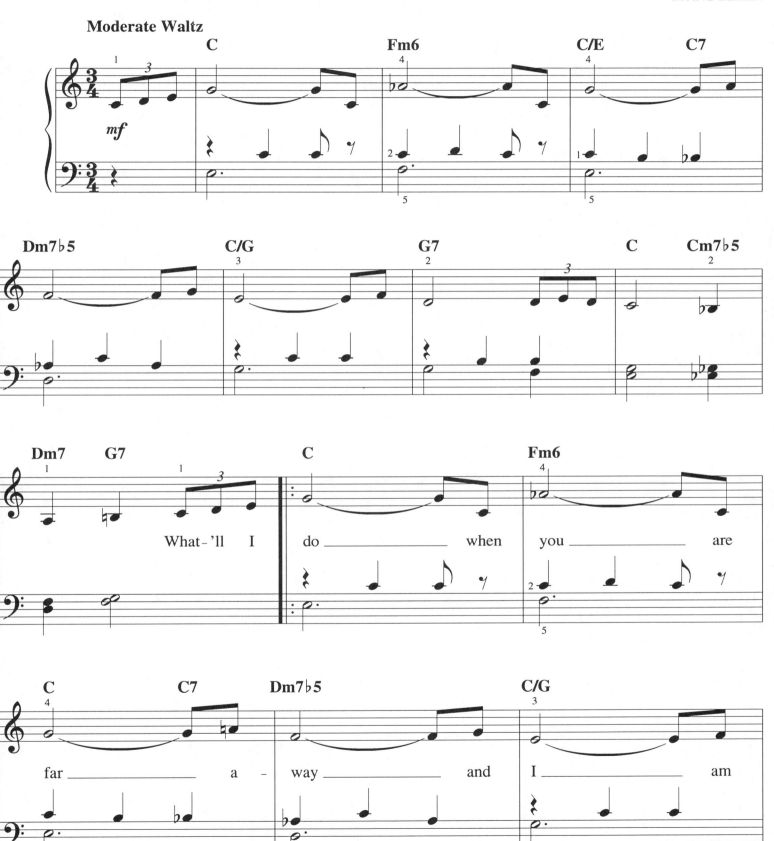

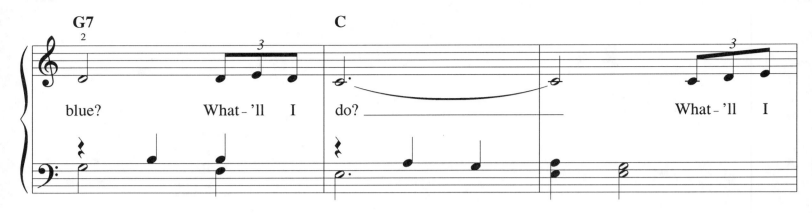

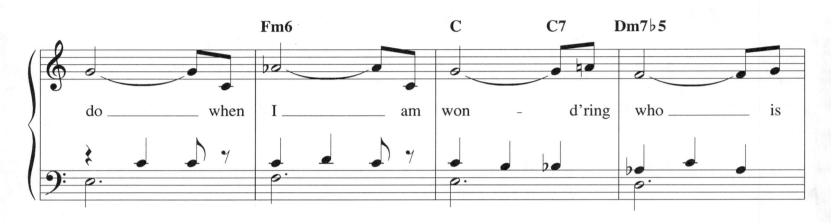

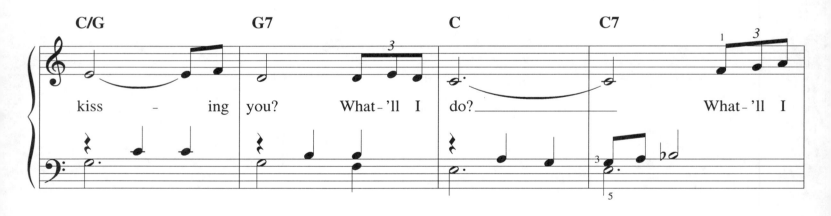

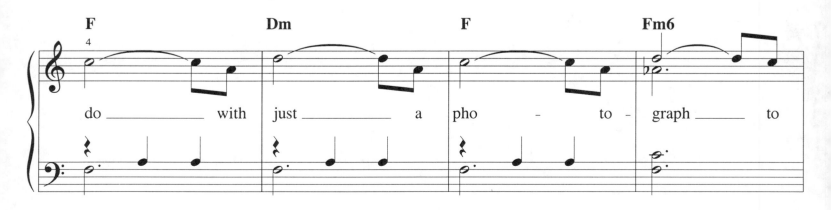

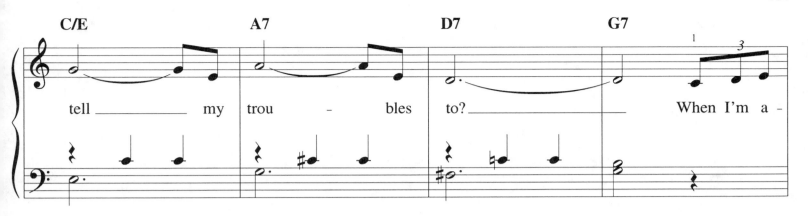

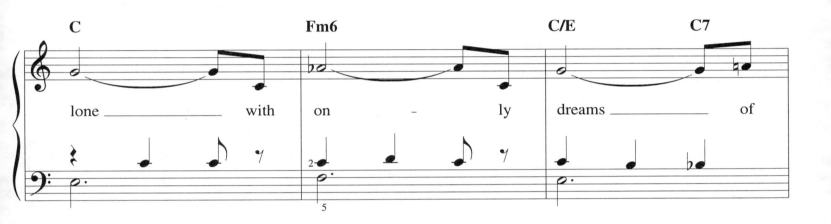

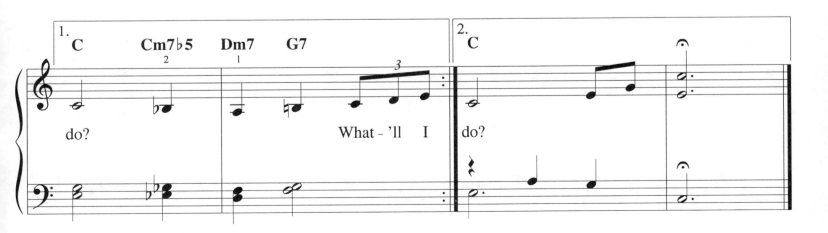

WHAT A DIFF'RENCE A DAY MADE

Lyric by STANLEY ADAMS
Music by MARIA GREVER

Slow Ballad

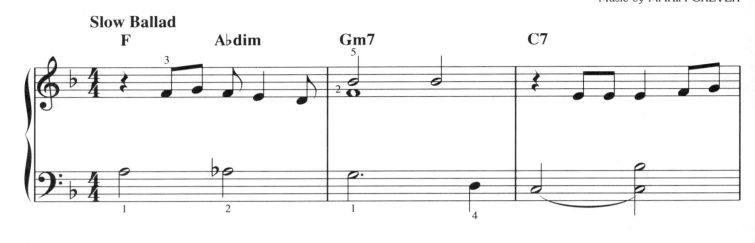

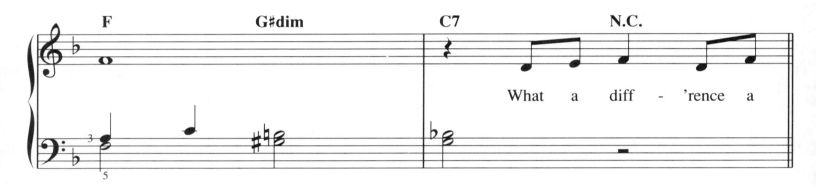

What a diff - 'rence a

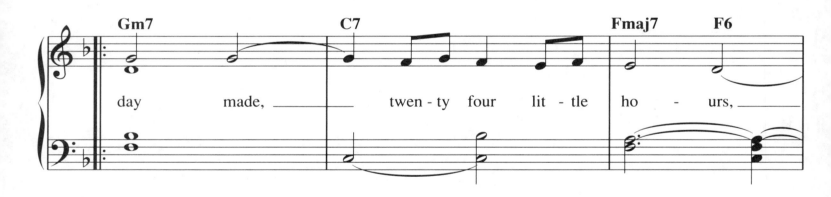

day   made, _____   twen - ty four lit - tle   ho - urs, _____

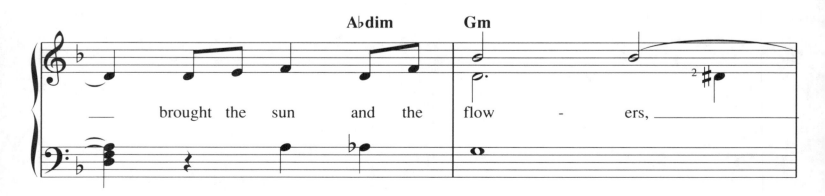

_____   brought the sun and the   flow - ers, _____

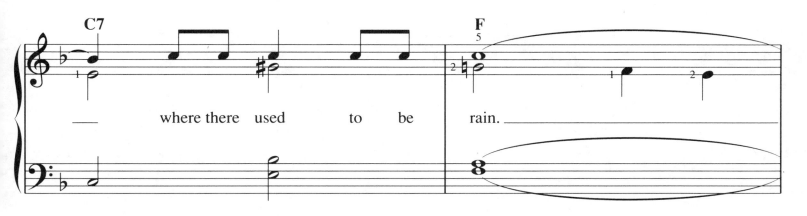

where there used to be rain.

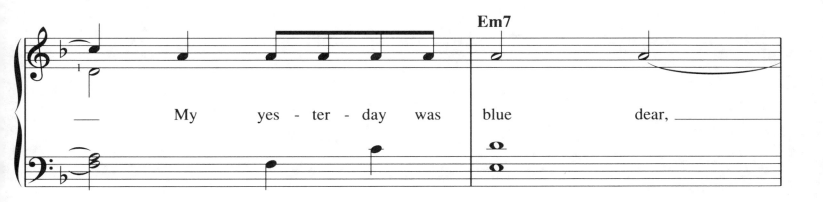

My yes - ter - day was blue dear,

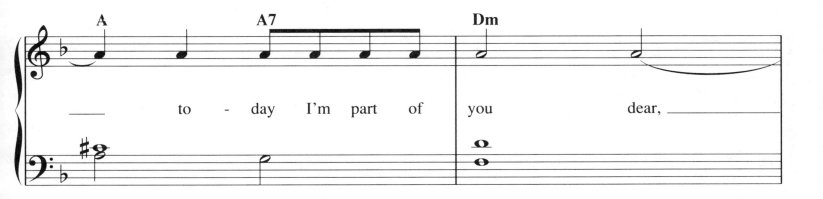

to - day I'm part of you dear,

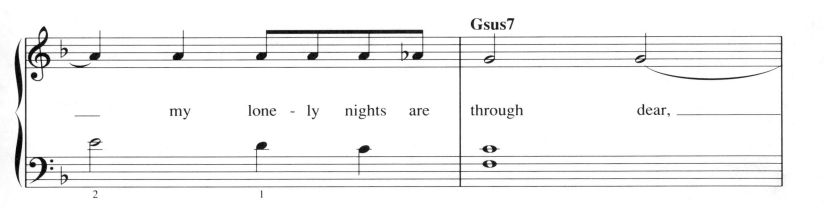

my lone - ly nights are through dear,

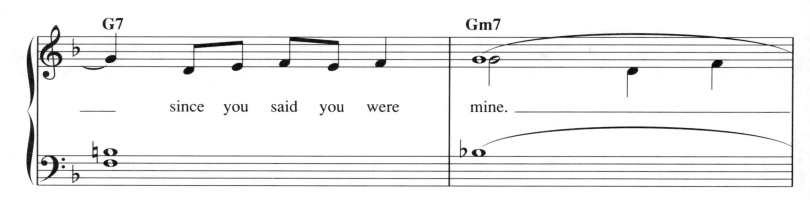

since you said you were mine. _____

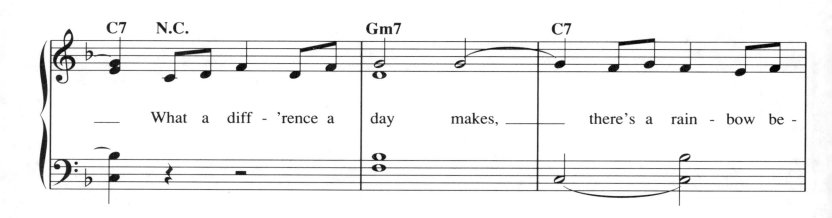

What a diff - 'rence a day makes, _____ there's a rain - bow be -

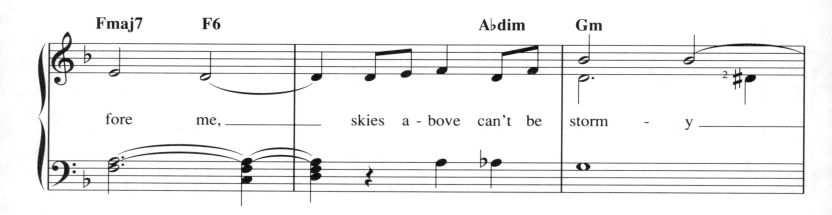

fore me, _____ skies a - bove can't be storm - y _____

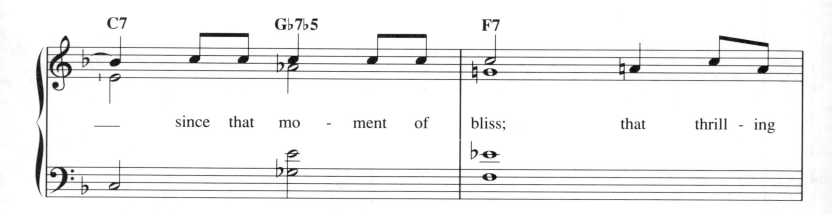

since that mo - ment of bliss; that thrill - ing

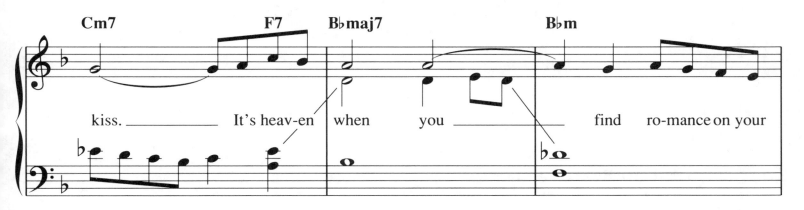

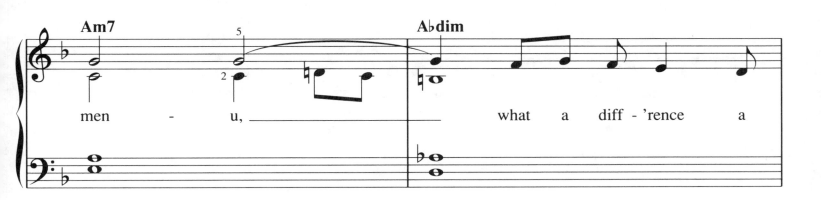

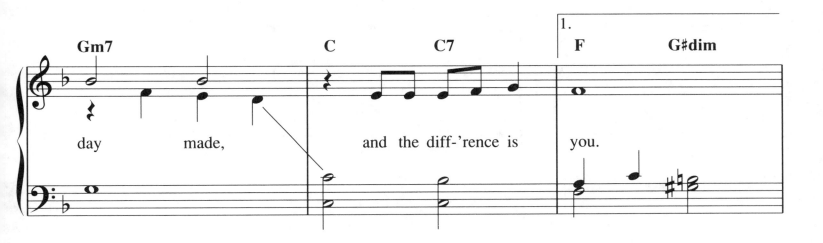

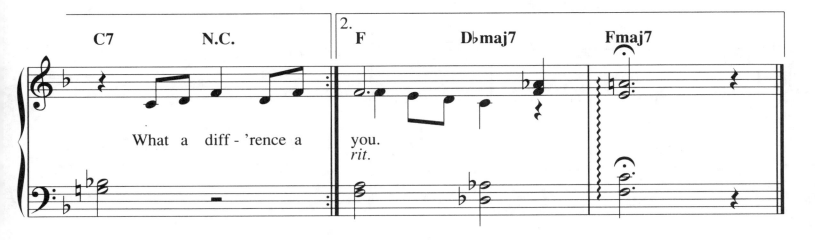

WHERE OR WHEN

from BABES IN ARMS

Words by LORENZ HART
Music by RICHARD RODGERS

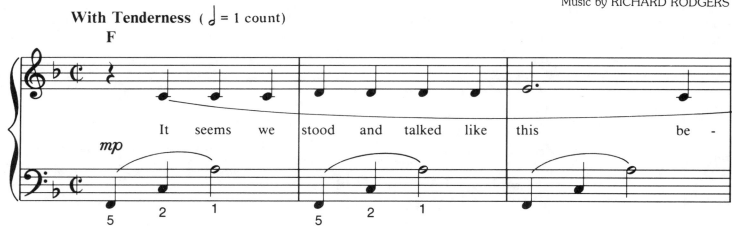

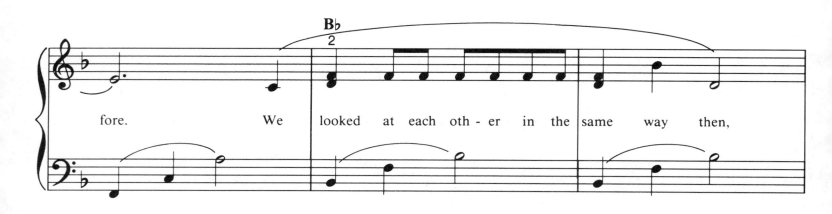

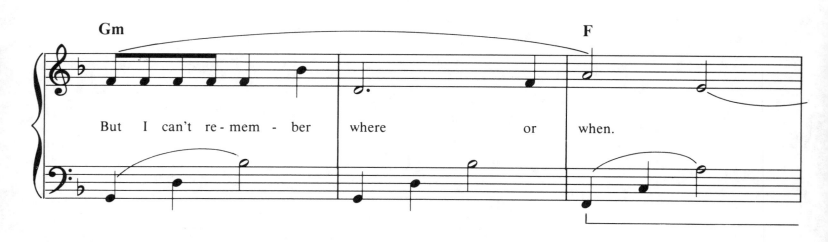

The clothes you're wear-ing are the clothes you

wore. The smile you are smil-ing you were smil-ing then,

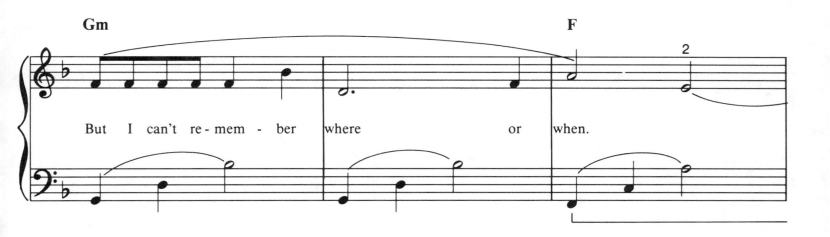

But I can't re-mem-ber where or when.

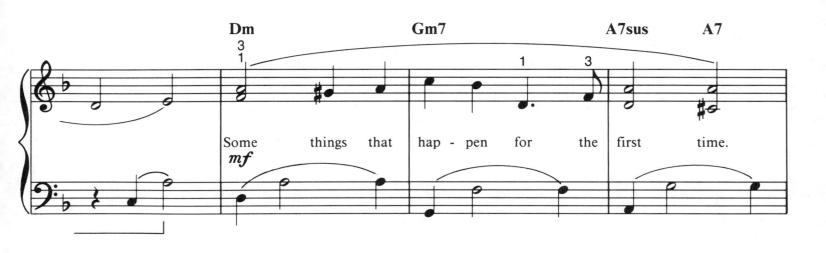

Some things that hap-pen for the first time.

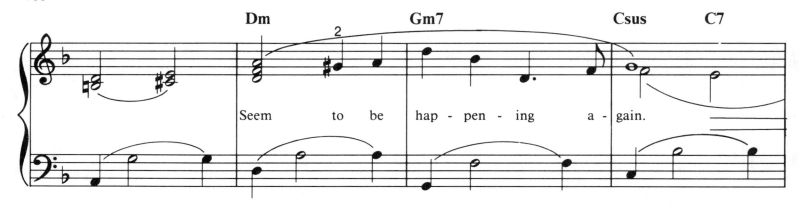

Seem to be hap - pen - ing a - gain.

And so it seems that we have met be -

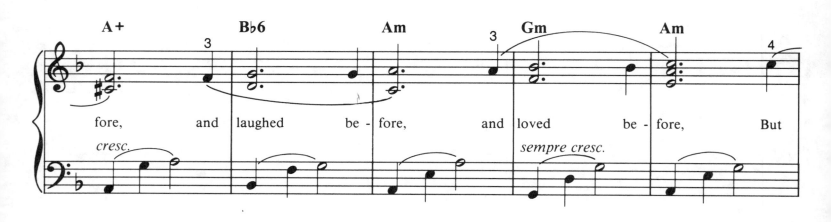

fore, and laughed be - fore, and loved be - fore, But

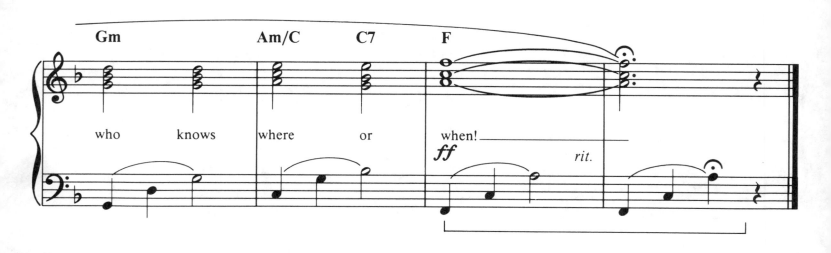

who knows where or when!

WITH A SONG IN MY HEART

from SPRING IS HERE

Words by LORENZ HART
Music by RICHARD RODGERS

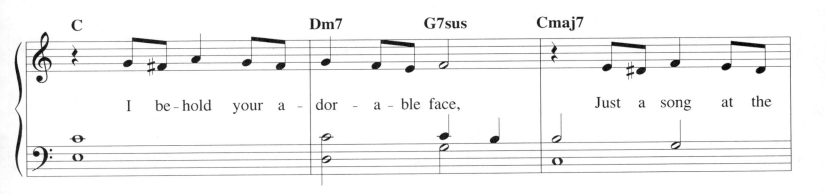

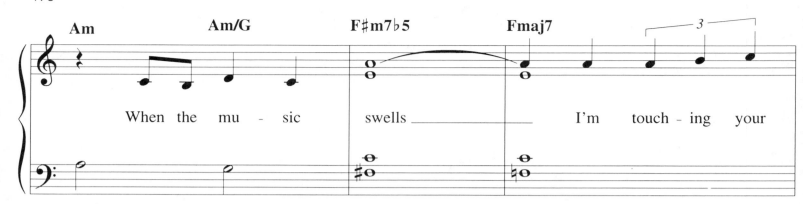

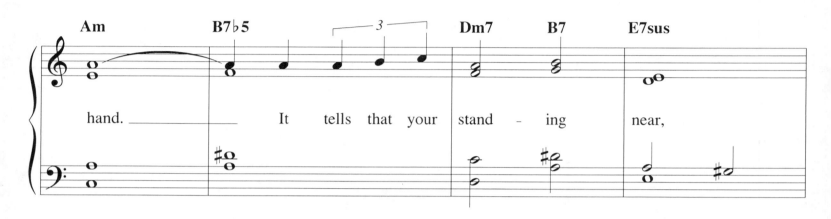

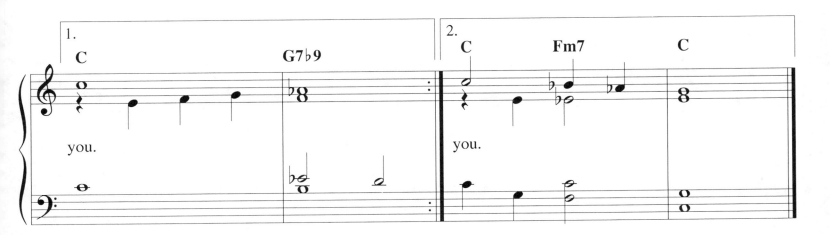

YOU BROUGHT A NEW KIND OF LOVE TO ME

from the Paramount Picture THE BIG POND

Words and Music by SAMMY FAIN,
IRVING KAHAL and PIERRE NORMAN

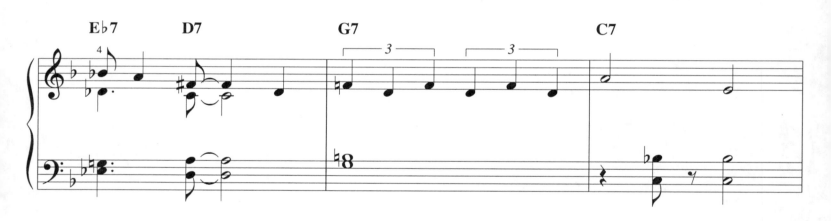

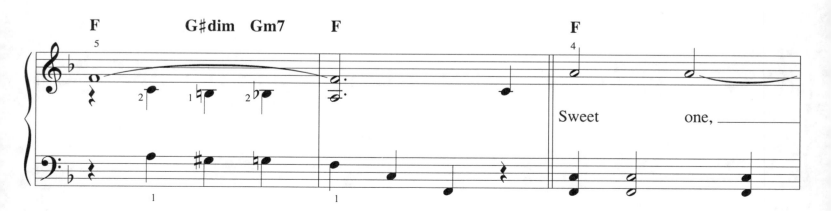

Sweet   one, ___

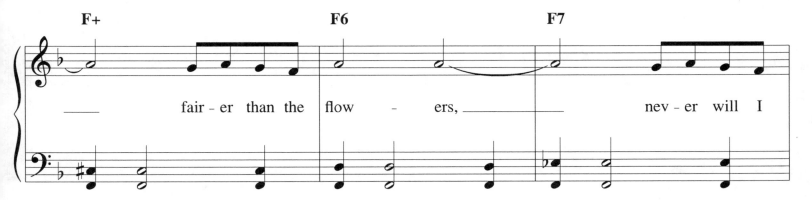

F+   **F6**   **F7**

fair - er than the flow - ers, _____ nev - er will I

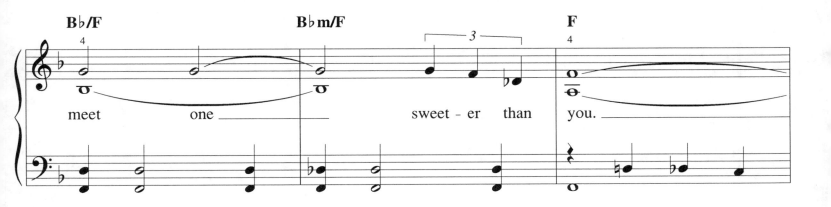

B♭/F   **B♭m/F**   **F**

meet one _____ sweet - er than you. _____

F+

Would you _____ turn a - way or

Dm6/F   **G9**

could you _____ real - ly learn to care if I'd ev - er

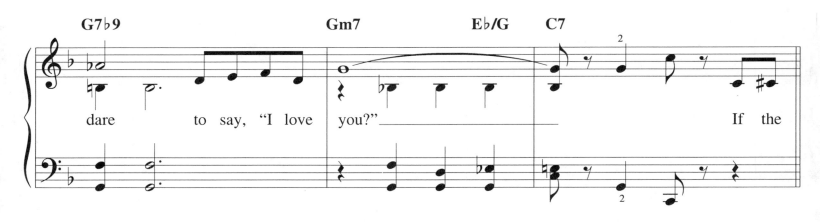

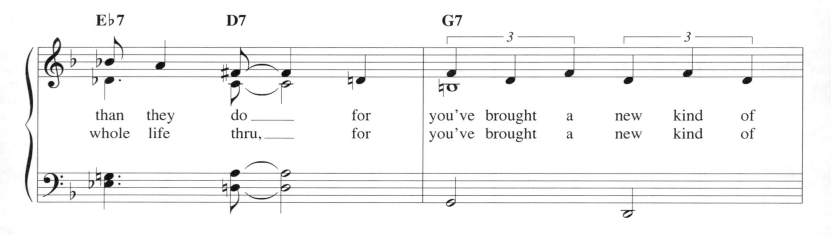

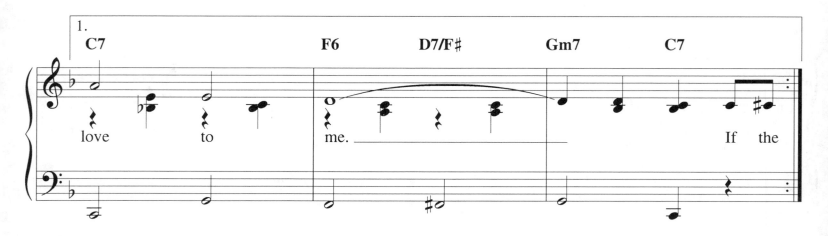

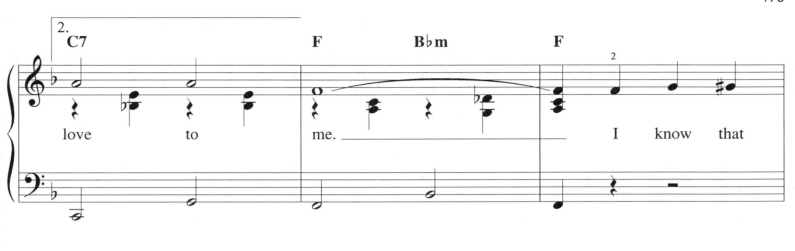

love   to   me. _____   I know that

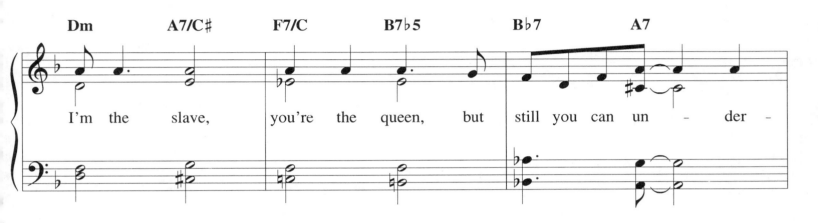

I'm   the   slave,   you're   the   queen,   but   still you can un - der -

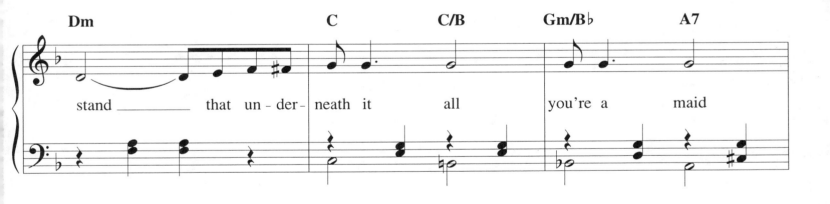

stand _____ that un - der- neath it   all   you're a   maid

and I am on - ly a   man. _____   I would work and   slave _   the

whole day thru, __ if I could hur – ry home to you, __ for

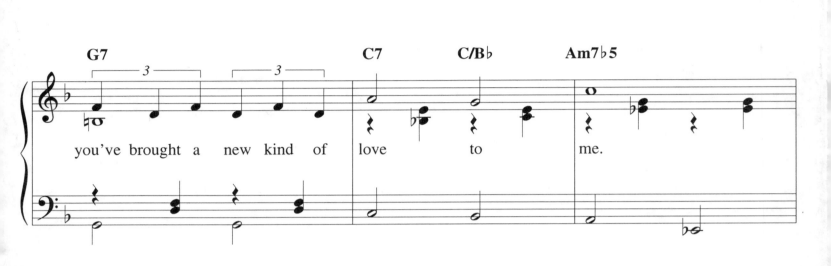

you've brought a new kind of love to me.

You've brought a new kind of love to

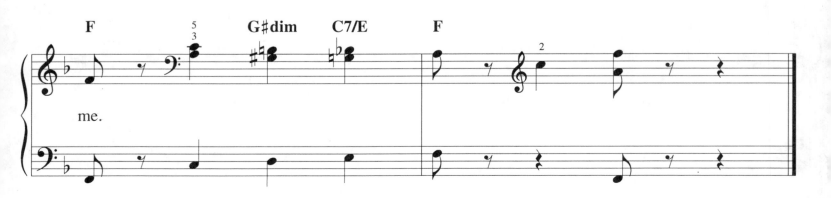

me.